Teaching the Post-16  KT-447-019

Resources in Education

Other titles in this Series:

Resources in Education

Teaching the Post-16 Learner:

A guide to planning, delivering and assessing learning

Marian Woolhouse
Trevor Jones and
Mary Rees

Northcote House

ISBN 0-7463-0926-0

British Library Cataloguing-in-Publication Data
A catalogue record for this book is available.

First edition 2001
Reprinted 2002
Reprinted 2004

First published in 2001 by Northcote House Publishers Ltd,
Horndon House, Horndon, Tavistock, Devon PL19 9NQ, United Kingdom.
Tel: +44 (0) 1822 810066. Fax: +44 (0) 1822 810034.

Typeset by PDQ Typesetting, Newcastle-under-Lyme
Printed and bound by Bell and Bain Ltd., Glasgow

Contents

1

Introduction

CHAPTER OUTLINE

This chapter introduces the book by explaining who it is for (1.1), how it can be used (1.3) and what it has to offer (1.4). Various terms used are defined (1.2) as is the overall model adopted (1.5). There is a brief overview of the background of the post-16 sector of education and training (1.6) together with some discussion of the Standards for Teaching and Supporting Learning in Further Education in England and Wales (1.7).

1.1 Who is this book for?

This book is for anyone who is a teacher or trainer of post-16 learners. This includes those who teach in further, adult or higher education and those involved in any kind of training within their own organisation. This might be in a designated role of 'trainer' or someone for whom training is an aspect of their job.

It is primarily for those who are new to teaching or training and need structured advice on working with the learners in their care. It presents, clearly, all the various aspects which need to be considered by the teacher, or trainer, with questions to be answered and tasks to be undertaken.

People come into teaching/training in this sector from a variety of backgrounds. Some may undertake the training of new employees within their department or section and this may, or may not, lead to more formal training responsibilities within the employing organisation. Some of these people realise that they are drawn to a career in teaching and seek employment teaching the skills they have themselves been using – this is a common reason for people entering teaching in further education colleges. Others begin by teaching part time, which may in turn lead to full-time employment.

The way you have entered into your teaching/training role is not important. What is important is that you understand as much as possible about that role and your learners.

1.2 Definition of terms

In this book the terms **teacher** and **teaching** are used to embrace all those involved with learners who are over the age of 16, whatever their role or title may be. In further education colleges, the title is probably 'lecturer', but with the changing emphasis in the structure of learning, you may be called 'tutor', 'facilitator', 'demonstrator' or a whole host of other titles. There are differences in what is expected of staff with these different titles, but essentially all are there to help people learn. In other organisations the term 'trainer' or 'mentor' may be used, but if you help others learn you can be classed as a teacher.

The **post-16 learner** is anyone undertaking any learning, at whatever level, who is over 16 years of age, i.e. over the age when schooling is compulsory. This could be a student taking a course in a college, a new recruit undertaking training before beginning a job or an employee who receives some training once employed. The variety is enormous both in age (16 to 60+) and also in the type of learning being undertaken. Throughout the book different examples are given to illustrate aspects being discussed, but it is impossible to describe the whole range of people who come under the term 'post-16 learner'.

TASK ONE

You may wish at this stage to define a 'typical' learner with whom you work.

1.3 Different uses for the material in this book

You can use this book before you begin your teaching or while you are engaged in it. The latter is more likely as few people undertake activities or training to prepare them for their role as a teacher (see 1.1 above).

You may want to start at the beginning and work your way through each chapter. However, it is possible to start at any part of the book if you have reached a stage in your work with learners where you need to know more about a particular aspect of the teaching/learning process.

You can use this book:

- on your own as a source of information about your teaching role – it is designed to take you through all aspects of the teaching/learning process (see section on overall model below)

- as an aid to a course or training programme you are undertaking in relation to your teaching role.

At the end of each chapter a list of references and further reading is given which you might find useful in following up or finding out more about an aspect of your teaching role which particularly interests you. This book is intended to be a starting point for your study of teaching and learning.

1.4 What this book has to offer

If your employing organisation offers support to help you in your new role, you should take advantage of this. Some organisations have extensive training for trainers before they are let loose with learners, while others offer only short induction programmes, allocation of a mentor to help you in the early stages of your teaching, or nothing at all. Whether or not you have the benefit of support from the organisation in which you work, this book will be of assistance by:

1. helping you find the answers to questions you may have about your teaching

2. providing tasks to help you better understand your role and the various aspects of teaching and learning.

Questions typically asked by new teachers

If you are using this book prior to, or at the very beginning, of your teaching career, there will almost certainly be questions which you are asking yourself about teaching and learning. In the box below, make a list of those which are of most pressing need for you to know now.

**TASK TWO – QUESTIONS I HAVE ABOUT TEACHING/
LEARNING**

The sort of questions you ask will vary according to:

- the stage you are at in your career as a teacher
- the stage in the learning process you are at with your learner(s).

Table 2.1 lists some typical questions which teachers new to the role ask, with suggestions for where you could find help in answering them within this book.

Questions you might ask with the answers	Chapter which will help you numbers	Page
How will I know what my learners are like?	Chapter 2 – Understanding learning and identifying the needs of your learners	10
How can I plan for an effective lesson?	Chapter 3 – Designing and evaluating your curriculum	34
How can I redesign my course?	Chapter 4 – Planning your teaching	76
How can I manage group work?	Chapter 5 – Managing learning	87
How will I mark the learners' work?	Chapter 6 – Assessing your learners	103
How can I evaluate my own performance?	Chapter 7 – Your continuing professional development	120

Table 2.1 Typical questions – and where to find the answers.

Tasks
In all the chapters there are tasks to help you think about your role and your teaching in relation to the aspect being considered. These are included to help you consider how what you have read about and learnt relates to your own teaching situation. You may want to do these tasks on paper or just use them to help you think about your response or reaction to the material being discussed.

1.5 A model for teaching and learning
The learning cycle is used as a model for teaching the post-16 learner. This involves a five-stage approach whereby a teacher:

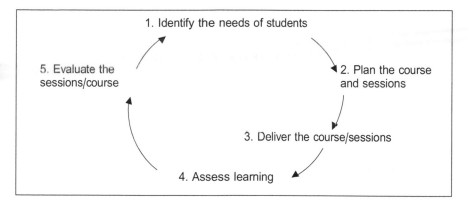

Figure 1.1 The learning cycle

1. identifies the needs of their learners
2. plans the course and sessions
3. delivers the course/sessions
4, assesses learning
5. evaluates the sessions/course (see Figure 1.1).

In some models you will see assessment and evaluation as one aspect, but there are differences between these, although assessment of learning provides useful information to enable you to evaluate a session or a course. This model is similar to that used in the FENTO Standards for Teachers and those Supporting Learning in Further Education – see section 1.7.

1.6 Background to the post-16 sector in England and Wales

This is very complex and it is not possible to list the entire provision, but an appreciation of the variety within the sector is useful. Post-16 education and training is provided in many different types of organisations including:

-   further education colleges
-   adult education colleges
-   higher education colleges
-   agricultural colleges
-   art colleges
-   tertiary colleges
-   sixth form colleges
-   universities
-   police service
-   health service
-   prisons
-   armed services
-   commercial companies.

In some cases – for example, in private companies or some public sector organisations – the education and training provided will be very specifically designed for the needs of that organisation, but in others there is a huge variety of both learners and courses of study. This is particularly true in the case of further, adult and higher education institutions, universities and prisons, but even in organisations which may appear to have a single focus there will be a variety. For example, within the police service, training is given to:

- new recruits
- those applying for promotion
- serving officers of all ranks
- support staff
- those engaged in the training of others.

Find out the variety of learners and (if appropriate) courses which are on offer in the organisation in which you work (see **Task Three**). This may be done by using the prospectus (if there is one) or talking to colleagues or the staff development or training office personnel.

TASK THREE

Courses   Different types of learner

This should demonstrate the variety of learners and courses to be found within the organisation in which you work. Of course, the people engaged in learning may not be called learners or students, but that is not important. It is the fact that they are engaged in learning, in some form, which is important.

The structure and governance of the various organisations within the post-16 sector is also complex. These aspects display a great deal of variety and are almost as numerous as the number of organisations involved in education and training. You should, however, try to familiarise yourself with the structure and administration of the organisation in which you work and also be aware of who is responsible for what within the organisation and how the learners you teach are financed. Some references for this are given at the end of the chapter.

1.7 National standards for teachers in the post-16 sector

If you read newspapers or watch television news you cannot have failed to know that all those who work in education and training are now much more accountable for their work. In schools there is a National Curriculum for pupils aged 5–16 and children are tested at key stages of this curriculum to assess the level they have reached. The training of school teachers is now governed by national standards which have to be demonstrated by anyone qualifying to teach in state schools. These teachers also have to continue their professional development using national standards and for anyone wishing to be a headteacher there is another set of national standards which have to be achieved.

In post-16 education and training there has never been the same amount of central control with regard to those who teach within the sector. Very few people train to teach prior to beginning teaching (although there are some courses available) – most undertake training to teach once they have begun teaching. Up until now it has not been compulsory to undertake any training or qualification to teach within the sector, although many organisations do provide training, or make it a condition of continued employment that the non-qualified person becomes qualified within a specified amount of time. The publication of a consultation document in February 2000 outlines the Department for Education and Employment's (DfEE) policy to make it compulsory for all full-time teachers in further education to undertake training and become qualified, probably within two years of being appointed. For those who work on a part-time basis, training and qualifications will also be compulsory but at a different level. Courses to enable teachers to become qualified will be offered within further education colleges, universities and other organisations.

The compulsory qualification will be based on the Further Education National Training Organisation (FENTO), of the Standards for Teaching and Supporting Learning in Further Education in England and Wales, published in January 1999. These standards now provide a framework for 'the FE teacher and those directly involved in supporting learning' and it is anticipated that all those new to this role will be required to demonstrate their achievement of these standards within a specified timescale of beginning employment within further education.

'Informing the standards... is a set of values:

- Reflective Practice
- Collegiality and Collaboration
- The Centrality of Learning and Learner Autonomy
- Entitlement, Equality and Inclusiveness' (FENTO, 1999)

which are designed to form a framework on which the standards are built and underpin any professional development using the standards.

The document also describes the key purpose of the further education teacher before outlining the standards. There are three main elements of the standards which are:

- professional knowledge and understanding (which includes domain-wide knowledge)
- skills and attributes
- Key Areas of teaching.

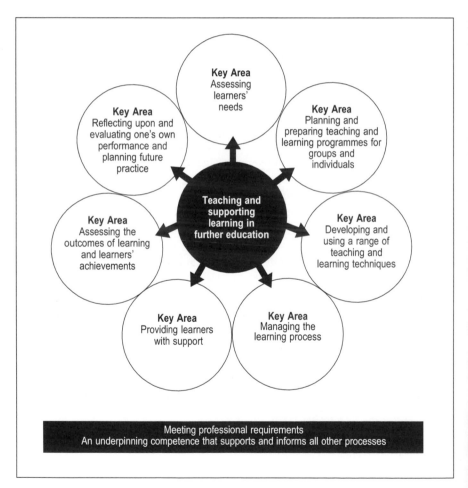

Figure 1.2 Seven Key Areas of teaching
Source: FENTO (1999)

There are seven Key Areas of teaching (plus Meeting Professional Requirements which are defined as 'underpinning competence that supports and informs all other processes'), each of which outlines the generic and essential knowledge needed, together with what 'teachers and teaching teams need to be able to do'. The **learner** is put at the centre of all that teachers do, as represented by Figure 1.2.

This book embraces these new standards by supporting their values, including the value that asserts that 'the ability of teachers to reflect on their practice...is crucial', and that reflective practice 'underpins the wider professional role of the teacher'. Throughout this book you are encouraged to think about what you have read and learnt and relate that to your own teaching situation and the relevance to your learners.

Each chapter contains a section where we suggest how the material in that chapter relates to the Key Areas and essential knowledge contained within the standards. You will not automatically achieve any of the standards simply by reading this book, but by completing the tasks and thinking about your role as a teacher you may gather some evidence which will help you to demonstrate your achievement of some of the standards.

While these standards are designed for those working in further education, they are valid for everyone working with post-16 learners in any situation. You may not be required to demonstrate you have achieved them, but they still form a useful framework in which to place your development as a teacher.

References and further reading

General
FENTO (1999) *Standards for Teaching and Supporting Learning in Further Education in England and Wales.* London: FENTO.

Structure and background to the post-16 sector
Armitage, A. *et al.* (1999) *Teaching and Training in Post-Compulsory Education.* Buckingham: Open University Press. (Chapter 9)
Huddleston, P. and Unwin, L. (2000) *Teaching and Learning in Further Education.* London: Routledge.
Reece, I. and Walker, S. (1994) *A Practical Guide to Teaching, Training and Learning.* Sunderland: Business Education Publishers. (Chapter 10)

2

Understanding Learning and Identifying the Needs of Your Learners

---

CHAPTER OUTLINE

As discussed in the introduction, learners in the post-16 sector include a wide diversity of people, and this means that the range and type of learner characteristics is correspondingly diverse, as are the factors which affect the nature and extent of learning.

In this chapter factors which may affect your learners are suggested and an introduction is given to some learning theories which may help you understand your own and others' learning.

Many of the learners in the post-16 sector will be operating as immature learners having recently left school, while others, an increasing proportion, will have extensive life and work experience and will prefer learning in a more autonomous way. In section 2.4 'andragogy' is defined as the art and science of teaching adults. A knowledge of the different types, levels and styles of learning can help you better understand your learners and enable you to enhance their learning. Section 2.5 will introduce you to some ways of considering individual differences in learning and, finally, in section 2.6 you will be encouraged to bring all you have learnt together and relate it to your own teaching.

The tasks included in this chapter will encourage you to formulate a profile of a group of learners to help you better identify their learning needs and how you can develop your teaching in response to your new understanding. It is suggested that you concentrate on one group for the exercises in this chapter. If your work is with an individual it can be just as valuable to construct a profile of that learner to help you understand his/her needs. This chapter is, however, written as if you are teaching a group of learners rather than an individual. You will also be invited to compile a list of general questions and answers to help you relate the material in this chapter to your own teaching situation.

The FENTO Standards addressed in this chapter

Many aspects of Key Area A – Assessing learners' needs – are addressed in this chapter. For example:

A1 Identify and plan for the needs of potential learners

(a) acknowledge the previous learning experiences and achievements of learners

(b) enable learners to review their past experiences in a way which reveals their strengths and needs

Critical understanding and essential knowledge:

- record-keeping
- accreditation of prior experience and learning, why it is important

A2 Make an initial assessment of learner needs

(a) consider and apply a range of assessment techniques

(f) assess the experience, capabilities and learning styles of individual learners in relation to the identified programme

Critical understanding and essential knowledge:

- appropriate assessment procedures for evaluating learners' potential to achieve the required learning outcomes
- ways of eliciting and evaluating learners' previous experiences in relation to programme requirements
- how to assess levels of commitment and personal characteristics relevant to a programme of study
- the differences in individuals' methods of learning

However, this chapter goes beyond the standards in Key Area A to enable you to continually revise your assessment of learner need and use a wide range of knowledge and skills to help you do this. Learning theories, as discussed in this chapter, form part of the domain wide knowledge in the standards as related to learning theory (d).

In addition, some aspects of Key Area H – Meeting professional requirements – are addressed in this chapter:

H1 Work within a professional value base

(b) acknowledge the diversity of learners' experience and support the development needs of individuals

(c) are open to different approaches and perspectives on teaching and learning

(f) ensure that their own practice promotes equality of opportunity and

---

addresses the needs of all learners

Critical understanding and essential knowledge:

● how to create an environment conducive to learning

2.1 Factors affecting learning

What is learning?
We should start by deciding what learning is. This has perplexed many researchers for hundreds of years. However, it is generally agreed that learning occurs whenever a person adopts new, or modifies existing, patterns of behaviour in a way which has some influence on future performance or attitudes.

Factors which affect learning fall into two categories – *external* or *internal* to the individual or group.

External factors
(a) *Factors which you may be able to control*
You may have some control over external factors which can affect the learning of your group. For example, the **environment** of the room and the **arrangement of furniture** to suit the strategy being used can be important. Most of us learn more effectively if we are in a comfortable environment. The image of the starving artist in a cold, damp and uncomfortable attic producing great works is just that – an image not a reality. Primary school teachers realise the importance of an environment conducive to learning and spend a lot of time creating it by, for example, displaying pupils' work. In secondary schools this is less prevalent and in most post-16 training environments it is non-existent. It can be difficult to have inviting classrooms when different rooms are used by the class and/or the teacher and when a room is being used by someone else immediately prior to you. Often the maintenance of rooms is poor – but most organisations have a procedure for reporting faulty equipment or facilities. You should find out what that is and report any defects. It may be necessary to follow up your report if nothing happens – but don't be deterred and don't assume that someone else has already reported it.

In most cases you can make a difference by ensuring that the **temperature** and the **ventilation** in the room are right (sometimes difficult as people have different 'right' temperatures/ventilation) and that the furniture, wherever possible, is moved to make the room inviting and to suit your chosen teaching and learning strategies.

It may be possible to change rooms if the one you have been allocated is not appropriate. Again, find out what the procedure is for booking or changing a room and don't be frightened to ask.

(b) *Factors which you may not be able to control*
These include things like the time of day of the class or incidents which have happened to the group or individual prior to your class. If your class:

- is the first one of the day and some, or many, learners arrive late, learning can be affected for both those who arrive late and their punctual classmates

- is after lunch and a group of adult learners has been to the pub, their learning is likely to be less effective than if you had taught them earlier in the day

- takes place in the evening and most of the learners come straight from work, they may be tired and/or hungry and therefore not as effective learners as they might be at other times

- takes place after a lesson with a teacher the class do not like, they are less likely to be well motivated to learn in your class.

By understanding the possible effects of external factors you can help minimise the adverse effect on learning by planning your lessons to take these into account.

TASK ONE – Questions for your profile of a group of learners

- What external factors might there be affecting my class?

- What can I do about these?

TASK TWO – Questions to ask concerning your role as a teacher

- How do I report defective equipment or facilities?

- How do I request a room change?

Internal factors

Much of the remainder of this chapter will look at the internal factors which affect the learning of groups and individuals. Internal means individual characteristics or personality traits that affect learning. This could also mean an individual personal difficulty, whether permanent or temporary. As the range and variety of learners in the post-16 sector increases there are likely to be more learners who are experiencing personal difficulties which may affect their learning.

If the personal problem is extreme, the learner may fail to attend, although in some cases attending a course can be the only stable factor in a life with much insecurity. The list of possible problems is endless, for example:

- break up of own or parents' marriage
- bereavement
- financial problems
- ill health of learner or close family member
- homelessness.

Most post-16 organisations have services to help learners with these, and many other, problems, but it is likely to be you who will identify that there is some difficulty facing a learner, or in whom he/she will first confide. This book is not designed to enable you to deal with complex counselling situations – these are best left to the professionals. However, if you notice a change in a learner's behaviour – for example, someone who:

- normally contributes to class discussions being silent
- is normally on time continually arriving late
- usually submits all work on time asking for an extension

you should ask to talk to that person after class or during the break. You cannot force him/her to talk to you, but by acknowledging that there is a change in behaviour or performance you may enable him/her to seek the appropriate help.

Knowing the services available for the learner to access in the organisation and within the local community will enable you to suggest how to help with specific problems. If the organisation in which you work has a student services department you can find out information from them about both internal and external services.

TASK THREE – Questions to ask concerning your role as a teacher

• What services are available in my organisation to help learners with problems?

• How can learners access these?

• What services are there available in the local community?

2.2 Learning theories

We now introduce some learning theories which should help you better understand learning – both your own and that of others. In the post-16 sector there has been a great deal of discussion and debate about the place of theory. The amount of theory, as opposed to practical work, you include in your own teaching will depend on the nature and type of course(s) you teach. You may have been involved in the debate within your own subject area about the place of theory. In recent years the use and consideration of theories to help understand learning in the post-16 sector have been marginalised by some.

We believe that an understanding of these theories is important and in this book we are encouraging you to consider theories about teaching and learning and relate them to your own teaching context. You should always do this as there is no right or wrong 'theory' about anything in education, although various theories come into, and then go out of, fashion. You need to assess the relevance and applicability of any theory as it relates to your own learners.

In this section we will look, briefly, at what the major branches of psychology have to say about learning:

• behaviourist
• neo-behaviourists
• gestalt
• cognitivists
• humanists.

If you wish to know more about any branch of learning theory discussed here, references are given at the end of the chapter to help you locate some sources.

Names associated with the **behaviourists** are Pavlov and Thorndike. From their work with animals, which showed that an animal would respond to an external stimulus, they concluded that human learning could be promoted in the same way.

Pavlov's experiments with dogs, where he induced salivation by giving the animal food and sounding a bell, is well known. When he removed the stimulus of the food and only sounded the bell, the dogs still salivated. Much of this work has now been shown to have little relevance to human learning at the level of formal education, but the Stimulus–Response (S–R) bond in learning is still thought by some to be relevant.

The **neo-behaviourists** such as Skinner, Tolman and Gagne developed the behaviourist model to be more applicable to human learning. They believed that learning should be broken down into its component parts, each part being taught and learnt in highly structured sequences. For each component part successfully learnt a reward would be given. This could be an external reward or simply a smile from the teacher to indicate success. Skinner was one of the first to develop 'programmed learning' where the teacher was replaced by a structured programme which corrected the learner and gave praise as appropriate. Early competence-based learning drew on this work by breaking down skills into their component parts.

Gestalt theory, from the German word for pattern or structure, is the belief that overall perception is important in learning and that learning is acquired by 'insight'. Gestalt theorists like Koffka, Kohler, Lewin and Werteimer, saw this sudden understanding of the pattern or structure as important in solving problems. They suggested that once this is acquired it can be applied to other situations the learner may encounter. Gestalt psychology has been criticised for its lack of proof or base in empirical evidence, although in some areas of the post-16 curriculum, insight and an overall understanding are important features of successful learning.

Cognitive psychologists believe that to understand behaviour it is necessary to know how people acquire their concepts and how these influence subsequent behaviour. The individual 'organism' interprets a 'stimulus' which leads to a 'response' (S–O–R). As each learner is different from his/her classmates, each response will be unique and different as each processes the new information or idea in relation to their previous knowledge and experiences. Dewey's writing suggests that the teacher is responsible for encouraging the learner to reflect on the newly acquired information/ideas and that learning is essentially a means of social growth. Others in this group include Bruner and Ausubel who advocated a more learner-centred approach and independent organisation of learning whereby individuals learn how to learn rather than learn facts, which will quickly be forgotten.

Finally the **humanist** view of education is that it should be about enabling learners to make choices for themselves and become more autonomous learners. Autonomy in learning will be discussed in section 2.4. Summerhill School, established by A.S. Neill, is an example of a private school utilising a totally humanistic approach to learning. In the post-16 sector an increasing number of courses promote a humanist view of learning, at least in part, encouraging learners to construct their own learning programme or have some influence/control over what they do and how they do it.

It is possible to see these 'theories' on a continuum with the behaviourists at one end and the humanists at the other. Although most teachers will favour one or two of these psychologies, in reality most teachers and courses employ a range of different methods associated with the different 'theories'. This is part of the professionalism of teaching – knowing what methods to use with which learners at what time. The various methods used in planning your teaching and managing the learning in your classroom will be covered in Chapters 4 and 5.

Undertaking **Task Four**, below, will encourage you to think about your own attitudes towards and beliefs about learning. There is no correct belief/attitude and your own may be influenced by the type of course you teach and your own educational experiences, both as a learner and as a teacher.

TASK FOUR – Questions to ask concerning your role as a teacher

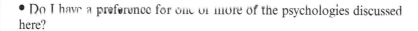 • Do I have a preference for one or more of the psychologies discussed here?

• If so, which?

• Why do I favour these?

2.3 Motivation

Motivation is an important aspect to consider in understanding learning, and in identifying learning needs and the appropriate teaching approaches to use. Motivation can be intrinsic or extrinsic.

Intrinsic motivation is where the individual wants to learn for the satisfaction of learning. This is often referred to as 'learning for its own sake'. **Extrinsic** motivation is where some factor, or factors, outside the individual is the reason for wanting to learn. It may be that the learner:

- needs the qualification for entry into a profession
- needs the qualification for promotion within their profession
- needs to complete the course to progress to a higher level course
- has been promised some kind of reward by a parent or an employer if s/he passes the course.

For many learners in the post-16 sector there will be a combination of intrinsic and extrinsic motivation. They will probably have an interest in the subject so want to learn more about it, but successful completion of the course, and gaining the qualification associated with it, will help them progress in their chosen career.

Recent developments in the post-16 sector encourage organisations to offer courses which have a vocational focus, so increasingly extrinsic motivation is the prime one for many learners – the motivation being to gain employment. You may not be able to change this, but in your planning and delivery of lessons you need to be aware of what motivates your learners, and it is important also to realise that you, the teacher, can be a motivating force. Most of us can identify a teacher in our own life who motivated us to learn and had a great influence on us.

Encouraging motivation requires that you pay great attention to the planning of your lessons. Teachers new to the role are often so concerned about the subject matter that they forget, or do not realise the importance of, planning their teaching and learning strategies to engage the learners and motivate them to want to learn. This process will be discussed in more detail in Chapter 4, but you should endeavour to make your material as interesting as possible by giving it relevance to the learners it is designed for. The nature and extent to which you can influence learners will depend on the individuals within the group, but you should be aware of your role in motivating (or demotivating) your learners.

Perhaps the most well-known theory of motivation is that of **Maslow** which has some relevance to formal educational settings. This can be easily found in any number of publications so will not be reproduced here.

It is recognised that positive reinforcement is much more effective than negative in motivating learners. So rewarding good work is more likely to motivate learners than punishment for poor work. Learners should have feedback as soon as possible after their work has been completed. It may not be possible to give it immediately, especially if it is complex written work, but you should indicate how soon feedback will be given on submitted work.

TASK FIVE – Questions for your profile of a group of learners

• What is the prime motivation for my learners?

• What kind of activities motivate my learners and why?

TASK SIX – Questions to ask concerning your role as a teacher

• What do I do in my classes to help motivate my learners?

• How could I improve what I do to motivate them?

2.4 Pedagogy and andragogy

Pedagogy is defined as being the **science of teaching** and is usually associated with teaching children and often used to describe what teachers do rather than how learners learn. Research in the area of child development has shown that children learn in different ways at different stages of their development and although individual differences do occur, a child progresses through different stages as their chronological age increases. Any observer of a child growing up cannot have failed to notice this. This book will not attempt to discuss the stages in child development, although it has been mentioned to illustrate that individuals learn differently at different ages and that adulthood is yet another stage. The study of how adults learn has been termed **andragogy**, to distinguish it from the study of how children learn.

One of the best known researchers in the field of adult education is Malcolm Knowles. He used, although did not invent, the term '**andragogy**', defined as **the art and science of teaching adults**, to describe his ideas about adult learning. He, and other researchers concerned with adult learning, tell us that adults learn in fundamentally different ways from children. This is why some school teachers working in the post-16 sector often have difficulties with these learners despite their extensive training to teach children and success in doing this.

As we have already discussed, the variety of learners in the post-16 sector is vast. They vary in:

- **age**, from 16 (or younger in some cases) to 60+
- **experience**, from having limited life and work experience to those who have vast and varied experience in many fields of work and life.

Teachers of adults must not ignore the experiences of their learners. Knowles said that it is the adult learner's most valuable resource.

How can one 'theory' be applicable to the 16-year-old school-leaver and the middle-aged unemployed manager? Knowles does not advocate that *one* theory is used for all adults in a learning situation, rather that we need, as teachers of adults, to make different assumptions about the nature of an adult learner from the assumptions made by teachers in schools.

Andragogical theory is based on a number of assumptions about the adult learner aimed at encouraging them to become more **self-directed** and more **responsible** for their own learning. The teacher has a different role in an andragogical classroom in that s/he should be helping learners to:

- make decisions about how to learn more effectively
- think about what they have learnt
- see how their learning relates to their goals and expectations
- become more involved in their own learning.

The extent to which aspects of andragogy can be developed within your classroom will depend on a number of factors including:

- the type and content of the course
- the knowledge and experience of the teacher and his/her confidence to give some of the 'control' to the learners.

In many adult education settings, the teacher is seen as a facilitator, helping learners achieve their goals rather than dictating what should be learnt and how it should be taught. Courses which have highly prescribed curricula may not be able to offer this level of flexibility, but a teacher who is convinced of the advantages of treating adult learners as adults can introduce some aspects of andragogy into his/her classroom.

In some cases learners will be reluctant to take responsibility for their own learning. Their previous experiences of the education system has taught them that to be successful they must rely heavily on the teacher. This is often the case even with adults who have vast and varied life and work experience but have not been in an educational setting for many years. Some learners may not value their own knowledge, skills or judgements. It is part of the role of the teacher, using an andragogical approach, to help them realise that their experiences are valuable and that they can begin to take more responsibility for their own learning.

TASK SEVEN – Questions for your profile of a group of learners

• What are the experiences of my learners?

• How much flexibility can learners have in this particular class?

• How can this be realised within the class setting?

TASK EIGHT – Question to ask concerning your role as a teacher

• What are my own feelings about giving up some 'control' within the class?

2.5 Identifying different domains, levels and styles of learning

There has been much research about different domains, levels and styles of learning that now we have many ways to discuss different aspects of learning. In this section we will look at three of these:

• Domains of learning – cognitive, affective and psycho-motor domains;
• Levels of learning – deep and surface learning;
• Individual learning styles.

When planning and delivering your teaching you should remember that these theories, or models have been developed as a response to particular situations. You should always analyse their usefulness to you in the context of your own teaching and remember that all learners are individuals and will have their own preferred ways of learning.

Domains of learning – cognitive, affective and psycho-motor domains

- The **cognitive** domain is to do with our thinking skills – being able to remember facts, explain concepts, understand patterns etc.

- In the **affective** domain we are concerned with attitudes. This area of learning is often neglected in much post-16 education and training, partly because it can be more difficult to assess than the other two, but it is considered important by many employers and is increasingly being built into courses.

- **Psycho-motor** skills are concerned with practical abilities and manual dexterity. Although there is usually some knowledge required, this domain is primarily about being able to do something; for example, drive a car.

While each lesson you teach is likely to favour one domain, much of the teaching we do in the post-16 sector involves learning in more than one domain. So, for example, in police training the officer who can administer a breathalyser effectively also needs to know the laws relating to drinking and driving and when to apply them as well as exercising appropriate interpersonal skills in his/her dealings with the public. A session concerned with this would therefore involve all three domains – cognitive, affective and psycho-motor.

TASK NINE – Domains of learning Think of an example in your own teaching for each of the three domains of learning		
Cognitive	*Affective*	*Psycho-motor*

Levels within each domain

For each of these three domains there are increasingly difficult levels. Most of the teaching you do will be planned and organised to enable learners to move from the lower levels to the higher ones. Figure 2.1 is an overview of levels within each domain.

Cognitive	Affective	Psycho-motor
Evaluation	Characterising	Naturalisation
Synthesis	Organising	Articulation
Analysis	Valuing	Precision
Application	Responding	Manipulation
Comprehension	Receiving	Imitation
Knowledge		

Figure 2.1 Levels in each of the three domains of learning – from Bloom (cognitive), Krathwohl (affective) and Dave, in Simpson (psycho-motor)

The first step within the **cognitive** domain is knowing and memorising knowledge. Comprehension or understanding is then followed by an ability to apply the knowledge and to analyse new situations using that knowledge. Synthesis is when the learner is able to re-combine parts of knowledge to enable original thought and ideas to be formulated. Finally, evaluation occurs when the learner is able to make decisions and judgements based on previous knowledge and understanding in the way a GP diagnoses the symptoms of his/her patient.

The **affective** domain also has levels but these are based more on an increasing level of internalisation of the feeling or attitude. At the receiving level the learner is aware but passive in his/her understanding. This is followed by being able to act in an expected way while being supervised (responding), then by behaving in a consistent manner when not under supervision (valuing). Finally, the learner is committed to the values s/he has been displaying and the behaviour is consistent with the internalised values in the way a good teacher is committed to the organisation's equal opportunities policy.

Within the **psycho-motor** domain a learner would move from observing and imitating a skill to being able to perform from instruction rather than observation. With practice s/he would gain confidence and become more precise. Finally, the skill becomes automatic in the way a typist can touch-type with ease, speed and precision.

TASK TEN – Levels of learning

• Consider one session you have recently taught and decide which of the   above domains you are working in.

• For each of these analyse the level(s) at which you are working.

Analysing your teaching in this way (see **Task Ten**) can help provide a structured approach to a course, whereby you help learners move from one level to another.

Levels of learning – deep and surface learning

The concept of deep and surface learning is related to the levels we have discussed above. Surface learning is concerned with the lower levels detailed in Figure 2.1 while deep learning occurs when the higher levels are achieved and the learner has a real and deep understanding of the skill, knowledge or attitude.

In any class you will have some learners who are content to learn the minimum to pass the course while others will want to know all there is to know and will spend a great deal of time and energy in mastering the subject. While there are individual differences, the extent to which learners are required to be deep or surface learners can also be affected by the **assessment** and **teaching strategies** used.

Some courses – for example, those with final unseen examinations asking for recall of facts – encourage surface learning, while others – for example, when learners are assessed on problem-solving activities – encourage a deeper approach to learning. If the teaching strategies you employ include asking learners to write a lot of material from the board or overhead projector (OHP), without any discussion or consideration of what they have written, you will be encouraging a surface approach. However, if you engage in discussion and group work a deeper approach is being encouraged.

TASK ELEVEN – Questions to ask concerning your role as a teacher

• What depth of learning does the course I teach encourage?

• Is this because of the structure of the course assessment or the teaching styles employed?

Styles of learning

Finally this section will look at the concept of individual learning styles. You have probably noticed, in your own learning and that of others, that different people seem to learn in different ways. A number of researchers have looked at this and have found that there are individual differences in preferred learning styles.

David Kolb's (1984) work led him to develop a model of experiential learning which suggests that there are four styles based on the individual's preferred way of learning. His model is often represented as a cycle (see Figure 2.2). Don't worry about the terms used by Kolb   another way of describing the cycle is shown in Figure 2.3.

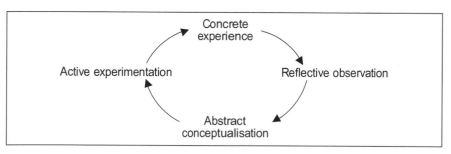

Figure 2.2 Kolb's cycle of experiential learning

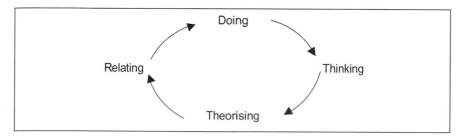

Figure 2.3 Simplified version of Kolb's cycle of experiential learning

Those people who prefer the **concrete experience (doing)** as a way of learning need to experience something in a real situation to be able to learn – for example, this type of person would have to actually experience at first hand tuning a car to be able to understand this aspect of engineering.

There are those individuals who learn best by **reflective observation (thinking)** so they can understand how, for example, to tune a car by watching a demonstration by someone else.

Some people are able to learn by knowing the **abstract concept (theory)** so that this type of person would understand how to tune a car by reading a book on the theory of the subject.

Lastly, those who prefer the **active experimentation (relating)** are those who only understand once they have had an opportunity to relate the theory to the practical work. So in our car-tuning example, they would only be able to do the job once they had understood the theory behind it and experienced the practical aspect.

According to **Honey and Mumford**, (1986) who developed a questionnaire to help people assess their preferred learning style, each person will favour one or more ways of learning which will put them in one of the four quadrants of the cycle (see Figure 2.4). The characteristics of the four styles are summarised in Figure 2.5.

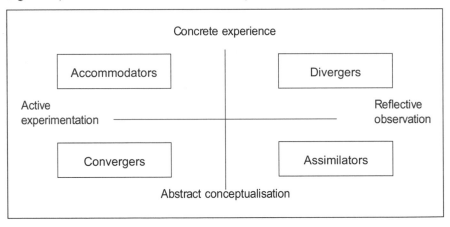

Figure 2.4 Preferred learning styles based on the work of Honey and Mumford

Kolb's work suggests that preference depends on the particular area of study a person has chosen to work in, or that someone with a particular preference will choose to work in an area which supports that kind of preference. However, others disagree with this and criticise this aspect of Kolb's work, as other studies have shown that the vocational area someone chooses is not dependent on the preferred learning style(s) they have.

So how can a knowledge and understanding of learning styles help you understand the learning of those with whom you work?

Accommodators	Divergers
• doing things/risk-takers • adapt to specific immediate circumstances • intuitive – good with people	• imaginative, emotive • view from many perspectives • broad cultural interests
Convergers	Assimilators
• practical application of ideas • things more important than people • physical science orientation	• create theoretical models • inductive reasoning – abstract concepts • theory is important

Figure 2.5. Characteristic of the different preferred learning styles

When learners evaluate courses there is often one, or a few, who seem to have had a totally different experience from the majority. This may be due (at least in part) to the teacher and the learner(s) having preferred learning styles which are in opposition to each other. There is evidence that as teachers our teaching tends to favour the learning style we ourselves have a preference for – see article by Dixon and Woolhouse (1996). As we are teachers we have, presumably, been successful learners, so we teach in the way we ourselves learnt, believing that to be the most effective way to learn. That's fine if all our learners, in all our classes, also favour the same style, but that is unlikely.

If you have the time and opportunity you can gauge your own and your learners' preferred learning styles by using a 'learning styles questionnaire'. Honey and Mumford have developed an 80-question questionnaire with a scoring sheet to enable individuals to assess their preferred style.

As a teacher you can assess your teaching style preference by completing and scoring the questionnaire developed by Dixon and Woolhouse (see Appendix). When using this with teachers in different vocational areas they found, not surprisingly, that teachers tend to have the same preferred learning and teaching styles, and also tend to use strategies which are best suited to their own preferred style. If you are interested in finding out more about this aspect of learning, full details of the references are provided at the end of the chapter.

Unless you are certain that all your learners have the same preferred learning style category (which is unlikely), you should try to vary teaching and learning strategies to incorporate aspects suitable for effective learning for all the different styles. Figure 2.6 gives an overview of how each style prefers to learn which can be used as a guide when planning your teaching.

Accommodators:	Divergers:
• learn best by doing and feeling • rely more on intuition than on analysis • need to know the practical application of knowledge	• learn best by undergoing experiences and reflecting on them • need to be personally involved • perceive information concretely and process it reflectively
Convergers:	Assimilators:
• learn best by doing • have a strong need to know how things work • need hands-on experience • enjoy problem-solving • are skills orientated.	• learn best by watching and thinking • feel most comfortable when theorising, developing models and hypotheses • perceive information abstractly and process reflectively

Figure 2.6 How each learning style prefers to learn (adapted from Lashley, 1995)

TASK TWELVE – Individual learning styles – Questions for your profile of a group of learners

•What is the range of preferred learning styles of the individuals within the group?

• What is my preferred teaching style?

• How can I adapt my teaching to help ensure all learners benefit from my teaching?

Another researcher in this field, **Graham Gibbs**, (1988) suggests that real learning only takes place when a learner has engaged in all four areas of the learning cycle. A learner can begin at any point on the cycle, although in many post-16 courses they begin with theory, but they must complete all aspects. Your teaching should be planned to ensure that this happens – not necessarily in every lesson.

For example, many learners are now engaged in work experience on employers' premises. Gibbs would argue that for real learning to take place, the learner would need not only to have the experience, but also to reflect on what they had learnt, apply their experience and reflection to the theories they have learnt in class, and then show improvement when they next have the opportunity to apply that knowledge.

An example of this could be on a childcare course where the teacher might discuss theories of child development with a group of trainee nursery nurses, and ask them to think about this in relation to dealing with children of different ages, before they embark on their first placement in a childcare setting. During or after the placement they should be encouraged to reflect on their experiences and assess how they have helped them understand the theories of child development.

TASK THIRTEEN – Coverage of learning cycle

Take one part of the curriculum you teach and do a similar exercise as the example relating to work experience.

* What parts of the learning cycle do you encourage?

* Are there some aspects which are not covered? If so which?

* How will you adapt your teaching to ensure that the cycle is completed?

Whatever part of the cycle you start at, you should try to ensure that it is completed within the course – not necessarily in every lesson.

There are other ways of measuring different learning styles, some work by responding to a computer programme which will give immediate feedback and suggestions for improving learning. Any can be beneficial if you use them to vary your teaching strategies to improve learning within your class.

2.6 Applying knowledge about learning in the design of teaching

All the knowledge you have gained in this chapter about theories, models and so on is worth nothing unless you are able to apply them to your own teaching to improve individual learning. In this final section we will look at practical ways of doing this.

The intention of this chapter has been to encourage you to draw up a 'profile' of a group of learners to identify their needs. To begin with, concentrate on one group – perhaps one which you have a lot of contact with. As you gain more experience you should try to do a similar exercise on all the groups you teach, although as your career progresses and you gain experience and confidence in your role as a teacher, you will do this more automatically. If you work with individual learners you should do this for them as individuals.

First you should outline the factual information about the group. This is important as it helps you to see all that information at a glance and also to recognise the differences between groups. You will not need to do all this if you work with individuals, although it may be useful to know what qualification, if any, they are working towards. The type of information you should include will cover:

1. course
2. name of group (may be the same as 1 but important if more than one group doing the same course)
3. number in group
4. age range within the group
5. gender mix
6. level of course/programme
7. stage in course/programme
8. subjects being taught
9. how this subject fits into the whole course/programme
10. attendance pattern.

The more difficult aspect of compiling a profile of your learners is to know their **characteristics** and **individual differences**. It may be that you will only get to know these aspects as the course progresses, but you can help yourself to know the group, or individual learner, better by finding out as much as you can before you begin to teach or as soon as possible after your first contact.

If you are working in a formal educational environment, the kind of things it is helpful to know can often be found in application forms, interview notes or information from colleagues if the group (or individuals within the group) are not new to the organisation. Some teachers deliberately don't want to know anything about their learners prior to their first contact as they like to give everyone a 'fresh' or new start. Your attitude to this will develop with experience, but it is suggested that those who are relatively new to teaching will benefit by knowing as much as possible as soon as possible. In this way you don't waste time planning lessons which are too difficult or too easy or introducing material for which the learners are not yet ready.

Throughout this chapter there have been a number of questions to ask yourself about your learners. If you collate the answers to these questions you will have a comprehensive profile of them, which will help you in planning and designing your teaching. Aspects of planning and designing your teaching will be discussed in greater detail in subsequent chapters.

In addition, you will soon get to know the following characteristics of the learners with whom you work:

• level of ability
• range of ability
• individual differences.

Some courses require certain entry qualifications (although you should beware of thinking that all learners who have the same qualifications will be of a similar ability) while others do not. All further education colleges now test full-time learners in literacy and numeracy (also known as 'communication' and 'application of number') during induction, which enables learning support to be offered if necessary. Some also extend this to some part-time learners. The precise arrangements for this will vary between organisations. It may, however, be some weeks before these induction tests are analysed and support given. Some teachers give their own tests to new classes to gain an idea of the level and range of abilities within the class.

You need to take all these factors into account when designing and planning your teaching as well as managing learning. These aspects of your role will be covered in more detail in the next three chapters, but you need to identify the learning needs of your learners first so you can best fit your teaching to these needs. The most important thing to remember is that:

---

all the learners in your class are individuals with their individual needs and expectations.

Summary

As a result of undertaking the tasks in this chapter you should have a profile of your learner(s) which consists of two aspects:

- factual information
- individual characteristics of the group.

The **factual information** can be gathered from documents etc. available in the organisation.

The **individual characteristics** of the group you will need to ascertain for yourself and a variety of methods can be used to do this. We have suggested that answering a number of questions about the learners is a good way of doing this:

- What external factors might there be affecting my class?
- What is the prime motivation for my learners?
- What are the experiences of my learners?
- How much flexibility can learners have in this particular class?
- What is the range of preferred learning styles of the individuals in my class?

This profile, together with the thinking and consideration you have engaged in regarding your role as a teacher and your attitudes towards teaching and learning, should enable you to plan, deliver and assess your learning as well as evaluate the course and your teaching. The following chapters will guide you through these processes.

References and further reading

General
FENTO (1999) *Standards for Teaching and Supporting Learning in Further Education in England and Wales.* London: FENTO.

Learning theories
Child, D. (1993) *Psychology and the Teacher.* London: Cassell.
Neill, A.S. (1990) *Summerhill: A Radical Approach to Child Rearing.* Harmondsworth: Penguin.

Motivation
Maslow, A.H. (1987) *Motivation and Personality.* London: Harper and Row.

Pedagogy and andragogy
Knowles, M. (1990) *The Adult Learner: a Neglected Species.* Houston: Gulf Publishing.

Domains of learning
Bloom, B.S. and Krathwohl, D.R. (1954) *A Taxonomy of Educational Objectives.* New York: Longman.
Dave, in Simpson, E.J., (1976) *The Classification of Educational Objectives: Psycho-Motor Domain.* University of Illinois.
Krathwohl, D.R. *et al.* (1964) *Taxonomy of Educational Objectives: Affective Domain.* New York: David McKay.

Individual learning styles
Dixon, T. and Woolhouse, M. (1996) The relationship between teachers' and learners' teaching and learning styles, *Journal of Further and Higher Education,* 20(3) Autumn pp. 15–22.
Gibbs, G. (1988) *Learning by Doing.* London: Further Education Unit.
Honey, P. and Mumford, A. (1986) *A Manual of Learning Styles.* Maidenhead: Peter Honey.
Kolb, D.A. (1984) *Experiential Learning – Experience as the Sources of Learning and Development.* Englewood Cliffs, New Jersey: Prentice Hall
Lashley, C. (1995) *Improving Study Skills. a Competence Approach.* London: Cassell.

3

Designing and Evaluating Your Curriculum

CHAPTER OUTLINE

This chapter explores the various definitions of the term 'curriculum'. In particular, four elements are worthy of attention:

- aims and objectives
- content (subject matter)
- teaching and learning techniques
- assessment and testing.

Other important aspects are:

- resources available
- the context or situation in which the curriculum is set
- evaluation (of the above elements and aspects).

Four models (emphases, approaches) are identified:

- objectives models
- process models
- content models
- cultural context models.

Each of these provides a different focus for our attention.

The sources of educational objectives are considered. Three different educational ideologies are useful in guiding us in the choice of objectives:

- the vocational training ideology
- the equal opportunities ideology
- the cultural heritage ideology.

The key principles underpinning the selection of content, and the choice of teaching/learning styles are reviewed, and then ways of evaluating the curriculum are suggested. Useful evaluative information can be collected through:

- survey evidence
- observational evidence
- documentary evidence
- statistical evidence.

Finally, aspects of curriculum innovation are outlined, including:

- types of innovation
- attitudes to innovation
- stages of innovation.

The FENTO Standards addressed in this chapter

Many aspects of Key Area B – Planning and preparing teaching and learning programmes for groups and individuals – are addressed in this chapter. For example:

B1 Identify the required outcomes of the learning programme

(a) interpret curriculum requirements in terms of syllabuses, objectives and schemes of work for learning programmes

(b) produce learning outcomes from programmes of study

(c) establish precise learning objectives and content

(d) define the subject knowledge, technical knowledge and skills required.

Critical understanding and essential knowledge:

- ways of establishing learning outcomes for programmes of study
- the content required to achieve particular learning outcomes
- how to analyse and evaluate skills, knowledge and values within a curriculum area

In addition, Key Area B (B2b) is addressed – select appropriate teaching techniques to accommodate different styles of learning.

An overview of curriculum innovation is provided, which is included in various parts of the standards.

3.1 Definitions of the curriculum

As with most terms in the field of education, there is no universally agreed definition for 'the curriculum'. The selection below reflects the range of interpretations:

- 'A course; especially a regular course of study at a school or university' (*Shorter Oxford Dictionary*).

- 'A curriculum then is concerned with prerequisites (antecedents, intentions), with transactions (what actually goes on in classrooms as the essential meanings are negotiated between teachers and taught, and worthwhile activities under-taken), and with outcomes (the knowledge and skill acquired by students, attitude changes, intended and unintended side effects etc.)' (Jenkins and Shipman, 1976).

- 'The "Curriculum" is a course of study followed by students at school or college' (Farrell, 1995).

- 'The amorphous product of generations of tinkering' (Taba, 1962).

- 'Curriculum is all the planned experiences which the learner may be exposed to in order to achieve the learning goals' (Rogers, 1986).

- 'The term "curriculum" has come to have a much broader connotation than it once had. Once it seemed to refer only to the content of educational provision and was thus barely distinguishable from terms like "syllabus" or even "timetable". One still finds it used in this way.... Many have recently come to prefer a definition of curriculum as all the activities planned by teachers whether formal or informal, compulsory or voluntary, within school/college hours or outside them' (Kelly, 1987).

- 'That the curriculum consists of content, teaching methods and purpose may in its rough and ready way be a sufficient definition with which to start. These three dimensions interacting are the operational curriculum' (Richmond, 1971).

- '"Course" is derived from the Latin verb *currere* ("to run"). "Curriculum", in its origins, referred to a running or a race course. The curriculum and its component courses provide a structure through which a student is guided by a process of instruction. Curriculum may refer to the composite array of learning experiences provided by an institution or department or to a fixed course of study (programme) leading to a certificate or degree' (Dressel, 1982).

Drawing upon this range of definitions, some important notions emerge about the curriculum:

- Systematic organisation and planning is important
- The content or subject matter is a key component
- Teaching/learning methods play an integral part
- Knowing whether or not specified goals and outcomes have been reached is necessary
- Constant change over time is inevitable.

TASK ONE

From your consideration of the collection of definitions, and your own experience of the courses you teach and have taught, what other elements play an important part in your definition of 'the curriculum'?

3.2 Curriculum planning models

The range of different definitions of the term 'curriculum' shows that it is a complex entity, made up of an array of various elements which may vary in their importance depending on the context in which the curriculum is delivered.

In order to simplify the complexity associated with 'the curriculum' and to enable you to plan your curriculum more effectively, it is helpful to have an awareness of different curriculum-planning models.

Models can be extremely useful in simplifying the real-world situation by identifying the key elements, components and factors which influence curriculum planning and therefore assist us in pinpointing which foci deserve most emphasis. They are frameworks or representations of reality which highlight the key aspects of a curriculum and show the interrelationships between the various parts which make up the whole entity.

So which curriculum-planning models can be of most help to you? Many classifications of models exist, but possibly the most helpful is a four-fold categorisation into:

1. objectives models
2. process models
3. content models
4. cultural context models.

These different types of models will now be briefly outlined.

Objectives models

One of the earliest pioneers of curriculum planning through the help of models was Bobbitt (1918, 1924), but the greatest interest came much later as a result of the classic book by Tyler (1949), *Basic Principles of Curriculum and Instruction*, where he posed four fundamental questions:

- What educational purposes should a course seek to attain?
- What educational experiences can be provided that are likely to attain these purposes?
- How can these educational experiences be effectively organised?
- How can we determine whether these purposes are being attained?

These four questions can be translated into the four questions which formed the basis for one of the earliest curriculum-planning models, Tyler's objectives model, namely:

- What are the aims and objectives of your curriculum?
- What is the most appropriate content or subject matter?
- What teaching and learning methods are most effective?
- What assessment methods can be used to determine whether or not the aims and objectives have been achieved?

These four key components of the curriculum (sometimes referred to as 'the four cardinal points') are closely interrelated and strongly influence one another. Tyler's views suggested that these four components could be logically arranged in a linear fashion (see Figure 3.1).

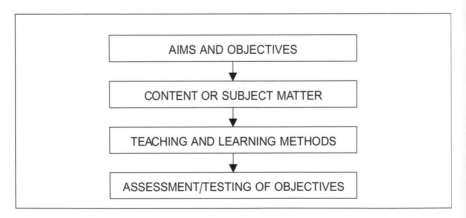

Figure 3.1 Tyler's objectives model of curriculum design

Tyler emphasised the importance of objectives in curriculum planning, hence his model or framework is often referred to as 'the objectives model'. Moreover, he stressed that objectives for a course should be very precisely defined, and stated in such a way that they are measurable and observable. He used the term 'behavioural objectives' as he maintained that, with such precisely defined objectives, it was possible to gauge the change in 'behaviour' of a learner as a course progressed. He maintained that it ought to be possible to identify, through testing, learners' knowledge at the end of a course compared to the beginning, and what changes in 'behaviour' had therefore resulted from the course and which objectives were or were not being achieved satisfactorily.

While aims are long-term targets expressed in more vague, general terms, often couched in a way which says what a course hopes to achieve (intention), objectives, according to Tyler, should be more precise, measurable and stated sufficiently clearly for the teacher to be able to assess whether or not they have been achieved. It is therefore important to state, as precisely as possible, what it is we require learners to do.

Therefore, 'action' verbs are helpful in writing objectives in some detail which convey the anticipated changes in the learner. Such verbs include the following:

list	compare	identify	demonstrate
choose	show	classify	divide
state	add	participate	move
increase	change	transfer	name
recognise	label	combine	justify
construct	order	illustrate	exemplify
describe	measure	contrast	define
display	mark	recall	evaluate

Examples of behavioural objectives, written in a precise, measurable manner, are:

- At the end of this course, the learner will be able to **draw** a diagram showing the working of a four-stroke engine.

- At the end of this course, the learner will be able to **define** the terms 'gross national product' and 'gross domestic product'.

- At the end of this course, the learner will be able to **contrast** the characteristics of coniferous trees with those of deciduous trees.

Tyler emphasised that the content of what is taught and the method by which it is taught are seen as a means to these behavioural, measurable objectives.

Many other writers have suggested curriculum-planning models in which objectives have been emphasised. Wheeler (1967) built into a design sequence some of the key points of Tyler's model, especially the prerequisite position of objectives and that the end result of education is to change behaviour. Wheeler did stress the interrelatedness of the various influences involved in curriculum planning (see Figure 3.2). It should be noted that although Wheeler called his model a 'curriculum process' model, by stressing the importance of objectives, it is different in type from the models considered later, where the emphasis is on 'processes' or 'experiences' encountered during a course.

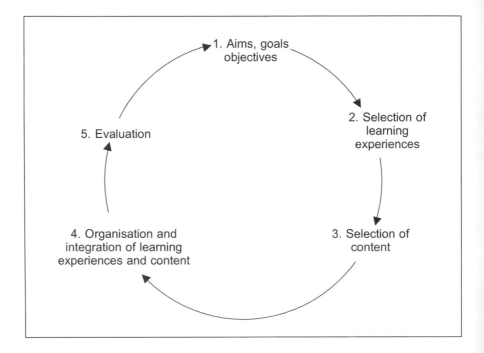

Figure 3.2 Wheeler's (1967) curriculum planning model

Kerr (1968) suggested a curriculum-planning model in which objectives were stressed, but which showed also the interplay of other factors, and noted that, in reality, the starting point for planning a curriculum need not necessarily be at the objectives stage, but could be at any of the other components shown in Figure 3.3.

Much of the discussion on the use of objectives revolves around the tightness of the wording of objectives, and a variety of labels have been attached to objectives indicating the degree of narrowness of the wording; for example, instructional objectives, general objectives, learning objectives, specific objectives, terminal objectives, teaching objectives, behavioural objectives etc. The debate often is over

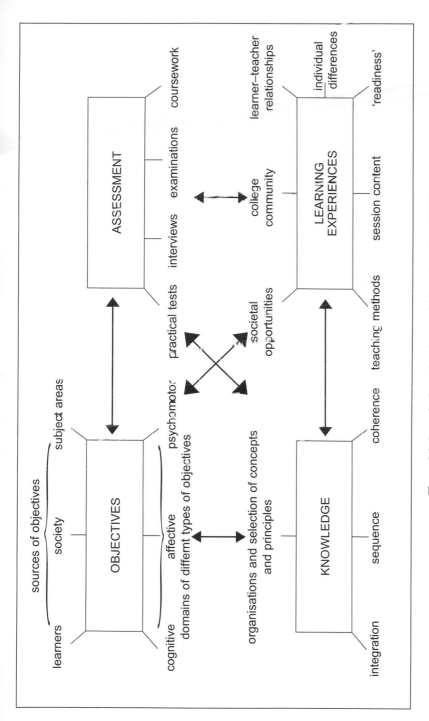

Figure 3.3 A curriculum-planning model based on Kerr (1968)

the use of language more than anything else; whether used in a tightly worded, measurable way, or more loosely, the specification of objectives in curriculum planning can be advantageous. Objectives can have the following benefits:

- They make it possible for teachers to communicate their intentions more clearly to colleagues and learners

- Where more than one teacher is involved in teaching a course, asking questions about objectives helps to bring aspects of the collaboration between teachers into more productive discussion

- They can provide the framework for the selection of course content and structure

- They can indicate the selection of the most appropriate teaching and learning methods

- They help the teacher (and learner) to determine the most relevant assessment and evaluation techniques

- They help to give a definite direction to a course, in aiding teachers to have views on what they think their learners should achieve by the end of a course, that they could not do before.

In writing objectives for your course it helps, as far as possible, to include the characteristics contained in the acronym SMART PICTURE:

Specific
Measurable
Attainable
Realistic
Time constrained

Positive
Individualistic
Clear
Transferable
Up to date
Relevant
Easily understood

TASK TWO

Think of a course you are involved with. Write five objectives which include the above attributes.

Taxonomies, or hierarchical arrangements, of objectives are helpful in illustrating how objectives can increase in complexity, and therefore such arrangements can act as a useful guide for determining the degree of difficulty of objectives as a course progresses in time.

The taxonomies devised by Bloom and Krathwohl (1954) and Krathwohl, Bloom and Masia, 1964) are the best known (see 2.5), but other helpful 'league tables' of objectives exist. For example, Ebel (1972) suggested the following hierarchy, ranging from the simple to the complex:

1. understanding terms
2. understanding facts, generalisations
3. ability to explain or illustrate
4. ability to calculate
5. ability to predict
6. ability to recommend an appropriate course of action
7. ability to evaluate.

Ausubel and Robinson (1969) proposed the following arrangement, again starting with the most simple:

1. rote learning
2. meaningful learning (the learning of concepts and principles)
3. application (applying a principle in new circumstances in a fairly direct way)
4. problem-solving
5. creativity (the use of relationships in the learner's mind to achieve a unique end-product).

The hierarchy proposed by Gagné (1975) is made up of eight 'types of learning':

1. Signal learning	} These relate to the pre-school stages of
2. Stimulus response learning	} learning.
3. Chain learning	}

4. Verbal association	} Approximately equatable with Ausubel's 'rote
5. Multiple discrimination	} learning'.

6. Concept learning   The ability to discriminate, to allocate objects to particular categories.

7. Principle learning   Involves the relating of two or more concepts with each other.

8. Problem-solving   The ability to combine concepts and principles and solve them in new situations.

All of these hierarchies help to give a structure to the use of objectives as a course develops. The benefits of using objectives have been considered, but there have been critics of the use of objectives, particularly where defined in a narrow, behavioural way. Macdonald-Ross (1973), Stenhouse (1975), Sockett (1976) and Hamilton *et al.* (1977) elaborate upon some of the problems of course planning which emphasises the use of objectives, and some of their criticisms are summarised below:

- Only the more trivial, unimportant, easily recognisable objectives are likely to be identified, while the really important outcomes of education, often difficult to measure, will be underemphasised.

- Pre-specification of precise outcomes may prevent the teacher from taking advantage of teaching opportunities unexpectedly occurring in the learning environment.

- Besides changes in learner behaviour, there are other types of educational outcomes which are important, such as changes in employer attitudes, the views of the teachers, community values etc.

- Measurability implies behaviour which can be objectively, mechanistically measured, hence there must be something dehumanising about the approach.

- It is undemocratic to plan precisely how the learner should behave after the completion of a course.

- It is rare for teachers to specify their goals in terms of measurable learner behaviours, so realistic expectations for teachers should be set.

Owing to these alleged shortcomings of behavioural objectives models as a basis for curriculum planning, some educationalists have suggested that a more appropriate basis for curriculum planning is to emphasise the process of learning rather than the product or outcome.

Process models

Curriculum-planning models in this category emphasise particularly the **procedures** and **processes** of teaching and learning rather than the **product** of learning, i.e. the learner's observable and measurable performance as pre-specified by behavioural objectives. Such an approach to curriculum planning has been favoured in the USA by Bruner (1960) and in the UK by Stenhouse (1975).

Some of the principles behind the process-oriented approach to curriculum planning include the following:

- The initiation and development in learners of a process of question-posing (the enquiry method).

- The development of the ability of learners to use a variety of sources of evidence in solving problems to suggest hypotheses and draw conclusions.

- The encouragement of learners to reflect on their own experiences.

- The promotion of open-ended discussions where definitive answers to many questions are not found.

- The creation of a new role for the teacher in which the latter is a facilitator, a resource rather than an authority.

Content models

These models emphasise the importance of **subject matter** or **content** in curriculum planning where the overriding purpose of the curriculum is to introduce the learner to a specific body of knowledge of distinctive information.

Peters (1966) and Hirst (1974) have been two of the chief proponents of focusing upon subject matter as a way of organising the curriculum. Hirst in particular proposed that there are seven **forms of knowledge** or disciplines or subjects, each with their own distinctive concepts, language, symbols, structures and procedures which represent the ways in which people experience and learn about the world. Hirst maintained that these seven particular forms of knowledge which should make up the backbone of the curriculum were:

- physical science
- mathematics
- history
- literature and fine arts
- moral education
- religious education
- philosophy.

Building upon these existing structures, newer subjects, termed by Hirst **fields of knowledge**, could be developed. The essential purpose of the curriculum, however, according to this view is to pass on the existing forms of knowledge, each with their distinctive characteristics, to form a firm foundation for further development.

Bruner (1960), although essentially favouring an approach to curriculum planning focusing on processes, did have some highly important points to make on curriculum planning through content, and developed the term 'the spiral curriculum'. By the spiral curriculum, Bruner maintained, learners would continually widen and deepen their understanding of the ideas of a subject:

> 'The foundations of any subject may be taught to anybody at any age in some form. Though the proposition may seem startling at first, its intent is to underscore an essential point often overlooked in the planning of curricula. It is that the basic ideas that lie at the heart of all science and the basic themes that give form to life and literature are as simple as they are powerful. To be in command of these basic ideas, to use them effectively, requires a continual deepening of one's understanding of them that comes from learning to use them in progressively more complex forms.' (Bruner, 1960, p. 12–13)

This interesting and valuable notion of **the spiral curriculum** is shown in Figure 3. 4.

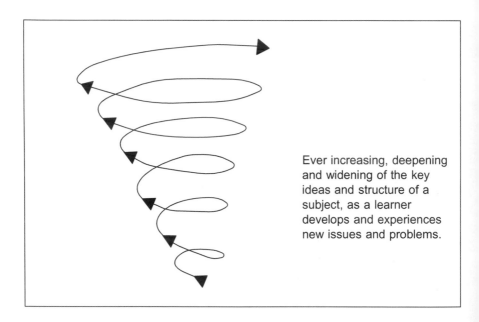

Ever increasing, deepening and widening of the key ideas and structure of a subject, as a learner develops and experiences new issues and problems.

Figure 3.4 The spiral curriculum

One of the great advantages of focusing upon content as an organiser for the curriculum is that it gives the teacher scope to analyse his/her particular subject, and to identify its specific ideas and concepts, its terminology, its methods, its particular information used.

Cultural context models

Two of the main proponents of this approach to curriculum planning are Skilbeck (1976) and Lawton (1983). This view emphasises the context or culture in which the curriculum exists, and the role of the curriculum to pass on the essential characteristics of a society's culture. Thus analysis of culture requires teachers to ask the following questions:

(a) What kind of society already exists?
(b) In what ways is it developing?
(c) How do its members appear to want it to develop?
(d) What kinds of values and principles will be involved in deciding on (c) and the educational means for achieving (c)?

(Lawton, 1983. p. 28)

In Lawton's (1983, p. 25) view, culture is:

'everything that is man-made in society: tools and technology, language and literature, music and art, science and mathematics, attitudes and values – in effect, the whole way of life of that society.'

Curriculum planners thus need to analyse and select from the culture the knowledge and experience most appropriate to meet the needs of learners and society.

Skilbeck (1976) emphasises that the culture of a college, university or other learning organisation is of dominant importance in fashioning the curriculum, and that in analysing the situation or culture of the college or educational organisation, factors relating both to the external and to the internal situation are of great influence. The essential features of Skilbeck's model has been outlined by Golby (1977) (see Figure 3.5). This model differs from the numerous models available in curriculum publications deriving from the Tyler rationale in at least four respects:

• It identifies the learning situation, not materials production and change strategies, as the major problematical area of curriculum development; encourages developers to think educationally about the situation which is to be changed, not about how to implement pre-designed models and techniques of change; and suggests, in a preliminary way, a number of relevant categories in the situation, to which teachers ought to be attending.

• It accepts that practitioners do not readily accept the command to 'specify your objectives', and encourages them to enter the model at whatever stage they wish

1. Situational analysis	
Review of the change situation	*Analysis of factors which constitute the situation*
a) External	(i) cultural and social changes and expectations including parental expectations, employer requirements, community assumptions and values, changing relationships (e.g. between teachers and learners and ideology)
	(ii) education system requirements and challenges, e.g. policy statements, examinations, local authority expectations or demands or pressures, curriculum projects, educational research
	(iii) the changing nature of the subject matter to be taught
	(iv) the potential contribution of teacher-support systems, e.g. teacher training colleges, research institutes etc.
	(v) flow of resources in the college
b) Internal	(i) learners' aptitudes, abilities and defined educational needs
	(ii) teachers' values, attitudes, skills, knowledge, experience, special strengths and weaknesses, roles
	(iii) college ethos and political structure: common assumptions and expectations including power distribution, authority relationships, methods of achieving conformity to norms and dealing with deviance
	(iv) material resources including plant, equipment, and potential for enhancing theses
	(v) perceived and felt problems and shortcomings in existing curriculum

2. Goal formulation

The statement of goals embraces teacher and learner actions (not necessarily manifest behaviour) including a statement of the kinds of learning outcomes which are anticipated. Goals 'derive' from the situation analysed in 1 only in the sense that they represent decisions to modify that situation in certain respects and judgements about the principal ways in which these modifications will occur. That is, goals imply and state preferences, values and judgements about due directions in which educational activities might go.

3. Programme building

(a) Design of teaching-learning activities: content, structure and method, scope, sequence.
(b) Means-materials, e.g. specification of kits, resource units, text materials etc.
(c) Design of appropriate institutional settings, e.g. laboratories, fieldwork, workshops.
(d) Personnel deployment and role definition, e.g. curriculum change as social change.
(e) Timetables and provisioning.

4. Interpretation and implementation

Problems of installing the curriculum change, e.g. in ongoing institutional setting where there may be a clash between old and new, resistance, confusion etc. In a design model, these must be anticipated, pass through a review of experience, analysis of relevant research and theory on innovation, and imaginative forecasting.

5. Monitoring, feedback, assessment, reconstruction

(a) Design of monitoring and communication systems.
(b) Preparation of assessment schedules.
(c) Problems of 'continuous' assessment.
(d) Reconstruction ensuring continuity of the process.

Figure 3.5 Skilbeck's situational analysis model (based on Golby, 1977)

e.g. the real problem as perceived by the teacher may be inadequate examinations, or poor text materials – either can be the starting point of developmental thinking.

• It is not committed to means–ends reasoning but accepts that an end – an objective, for example – is only meaningful in and through activity

• It makes no assumptions about the depth and scale of inquiries into any one of the stages identified beyond the basic point that effective and justifiable college-based curriculum development requires that criteria be formulated and colleges assisted in their endeavours to satisfy these criteria.

TASK THREE

Think of a course you are involved in teaching. To what extent do the (a) external and (b) internal elements identified in Skilbeck's model affect the design and delivery of that course?

Which factors are of greatest importance?

The hidden curriculum

As part of the analysis of the situation, culture or context in which the curriculum is taught, the concept of 'the hidden curriculum' is of considerable importance (Snyder, 1971; Apple, 1979). The idea refers to the values, attitudes, norms, perceptions and terminology communicated to the learner, either intentionally or unintentionally, which are not made explicit in the official or formal curriculum.

How quickly learners find their way around these hidden rules, norms, procedures and values can have considerable impact on their relationship with the teacher and other learners, and their enjoyment and success in learning. It is, therefore, helpful to try to make the various hidden values, norms, procedures etc. as visible as possible to learners; in other words, to attempt to make the actual or received curriculum as close as possible to the planned or intended curriculum. For example, if there is variation in the use of first name terms between teachers and learners, it is of help to clarify your expectations about this at the outset of a course.

Similar variations exist in the punctuality expected and tolerated. Some teachers may not allow entry to a class more than five minutes after the beginning of a learning session, while others may have a more tolerant attitude and arrangement. Again, rules on punctuality may vary between courses where the learners are on full-time and part-time courses. Different teachers may respond with different degrees of leniency to submission dates for coursework. So it helps to clarify attitudes, interpretations of official rules and requirements etc. as soon as possible, rather than leaving the student to guess, often with unfortunate consequences, his/her way through a difficult maze of covert norms and expectations.

TASK FOUR

Think of a course you are involved with. Identify the aspects which could be hidden to learners.

Consider the various ways in which these hidden elements can be made more open and less ambiguous.

Are there any problems in attempting to demystify the hidden curriculum?

A composite model
A helpful approach to curriculum planning is to merge the four different types of model, the objectives model, the process model, the content model and the cultural context model, into one composite model which identifies the key elements of each type. Such a framework is shown in Figure 3.6.

3.3 Sources of educational objectives
However narrowly or precisely objectives are stated, most agree that it is of help to both teachers and learners to have a direction, goal and purpose to aim for in

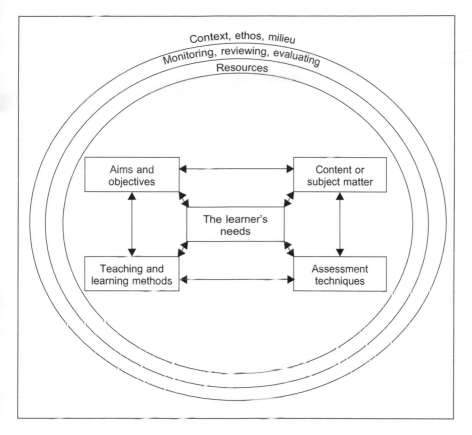

Figure 3.6 A composite model of curriculum design, showing the
various elements influencing the planning process

educational experiences. Even the simplest of courses will have a range of different
objectives, and so the clarification of the sources of objectives does have the
advantage of preventing possible conflict between these objectives.

A useful way of clarifying sources of objectives is to examine different **ideologies**,
or sets of values, or approaches, or viewpoints, to determine where possible
conflicts may arise in objectives. A variety of different ideologies exist, but a
threefold division is helpful, as shown in Fig 3.7.

In Figure 3.7 the different ideologies have been shown in equal area circles with
no overlap. In reality, when objectives are chosen from the different perspectives,
the emphasis will be greater in one area and may, unless care is taken, conflict with
objectives from one or more of the other ideologies, since each perspective has its
own set of values and characteristics.

What are the different features associated with each viewpoint?

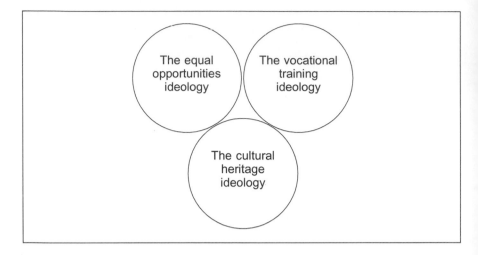

Figure 3.7 Different educational ideologies or sets of values behind the post-16 curriculum

The vocational training ideology
- Education is seen as the means of providing appropriate skills and knowledge which will contribute to the creation of economic wealth.
- Technological innovation is particularly valued; for example, computer-aided learning.
- Teaching encourages habits of punctuality, self-discipline, obedience and competitiveness.
- League tables are important, based on various performance indicators such as examination pass rates and learner success rates in finding future employment.
- Industrial management concepts, such as income generation and performance-based pay, are prized.

The cultural heritage ideology
- Transmission of traditional culture by authoritative teachers is key.
- Teaching should concentrate on subjects which are traditionally valued and have a perceived high status.
- The acquisition of worthwhile knowledge is paramount, as is the maintenance of academic standards and the process of passing on a culture from one generation to the next.
- Formal relationships between teacher and learner are more likely.
- Traditional teaching styles are more evident.
- Rigorous entry qualifications to courses are emphasised.

- Assessment is by examination rather than by coursework.

The equal opportunities ideology
- Education is valued as a means of redressing inequalities in society.
- Learners should have equal chances of success in education (and life) through their own endeavours, irrespective of wealth, gender or ethnic group.
- Access to courses is as open as possible.
- The emphasis is placed on learner-centred education, individual performance, collaboration and democratic processes in learning.
- Self- and peer-assessment are important, with coursework favoured in place of examinations.
- The teacher is more a facilitator and learns with the learners, rather than an authority figure.
- The focus is on problem-solving, creativity, critical thinking and education of attitudes and emotions.

The above points summarise the ideologies, and more detailed views are provided by Scrimshaw (1983) and Kelly (1987).

The ideal situation in practice, of course, is to ensure that where sources of objectives are from a different ideological area, as little conflict as possible between the objectives prevails.

TASK FIVE

Consider a course which you teach. Which educational ideology takes priority in shaping its objectives?

Do all parts of the course, some of which may be taught by other teaching colleagues, have the same ideological priority?

If there are differences in priority, what difficulties may arise?

How can these problems be alleviated?

It is helpful to explain to the learner at the outset what educational viewpoint the course emphasises and where different parts of a course – for example, optional choices – have different educational perspectives. The learner may then be more aware of the reasons for a shift in emphasis in objectives (and indeed other elements of the course such as content, teaching styles, assessment methods and resources).

3.4 Selection of content

In some instances, the content of a course is prescribed in some detail in various course documents and syllabuses from 'external' bodies such as examination boards. In other cases, there may be very little guidance on what subject matter has to be taught.

Whatever the particular context is in your teaching situation, it is helpful to have some guidelines for the selection, structuring and sequencing of content or subject matter. Below are some useful pointers, which are very closely interrelated:

- *Start with what your learners know and progress to the unknown.* This means that it is essential to try to find out at the beginning of a course what your learners already know. This may seem obvious, but even on courses where there are prescribed entry requirements, the variations among learners in what they know may be wide. (See Chapter 2.)

  The advantage of starting with the familiar and progressing to the unfamiliar is the confidence it promotes in your learners. The opposite, of being plunged into a totally unfamiliar area of knowledge, is off-putting and disconcerting, and is one of the reasons for the early drop-out of learners from some courses.

  How you establish what your learners know at the outset is not an easy task, especially with large groups, but discussion, simple tests and observation in practical areas are some of the ways of determining such knowledge at the outset.

- *Put the subject matter in context*, to give a clear indication of how it fits into an overall pattern. Thus before focusing on the detailed parts, give a coherent picture of the whole.

- *Progress from simple subject matter towards the more complex.* Try to analyse the key concepts, ideas and terminology of the subject matter being taught and split these down into simplified components or elements. As the course progresses, these elements can be constantly revisited and refined and developed, interrelationships between them can be shown, and an overall, coherent picture of the body of knowledge can be built up.

  The idea of the spiral curriculum (Figure 3.4) is helpful in the development of subject matter in which the key ideas are constantly developed from simple fundamentals.

- *Proceed from concrete, tangible content towards the more abstract and theoretical notions.* Very often this entails observation, practice of skills connected with the subject matter which progresses towards reasoning and theoretical understanding.

- *Try to relate the subject matter to the learners' experiences.* One of the advantages of teaching the post-16 context is the varied experience of the learners. If you focus upon the learners' experiences, the content becomes more meaningful, and interrelationships with other subject matter is more easily recognised.

- *Deal with small, manageable amounts of subject material, rather than 'trying to cover everything'.* One of the most common reasons why some learners do not succeed is overload of information by the teacher. A thoughtful breakdown of the key ideas and issues of a particular subject area is usually of much greater benefit to the learner than very large amounts of factual detail that cannot be absorbed. Even with large, detailed, prescriptive syllabuses, only a skeleton outline of the really important principles, used and developed in an interesting and challenging way, is necessary. Sometimes the learners themselves, particularly the more mature ones, will be able to suggest what they think the key areas to be covered should be.

- *Make the content 'active' rather than 'passive'.* This entails the judicious use of resources; for example, the setting of problem-solving exercises and tasks based on materials given to the learners. In this way, learners can appreciate why and how far the subject matter is useful and relevant, rather than seeing it in a void or isolated, less meaningful vacuum.

- *Continuity of subject material is more effective than unconnected episodes.* It is important to show and reinforce links between subject matter focused upon with previous and future work, and, in some cases, content in other contexts.

- *Select subject matter which offers the maximum opportunity to the learners to succeed.* Learners progress more effectively if they know they can succeed in a certain area of knowledge. Nothing is more daunting to a learner than failure (or the fear of failure), and subject matter associated with success results in enjoyable, effective, enthusiastic learners. Therefore feedback given to learners as soon as possible is vital for learning success.

3.5 Choice of teaching styles

This section outlines some of the rules of thumb which can help decisions about choice of teaching style. It is helpful to bear in mind always the key elements involved in the choice of teaching styles, namely the needs of the learner, the context, the aims and objectives of the course, subject matter, assessment techniques and resources available (see Figure 3.6), and to recognise the close interplay of these factors. It is also important to appreciate that teaching and learning can be considered as part of a continuum where the focus is sometimes on the learner, sometimes on the teacher at different periods of a course, or indeed teaching session (Figure 3.8). Most recognise that many learners (probably most) learn most effectively when actively involved in the learning-teaching process.

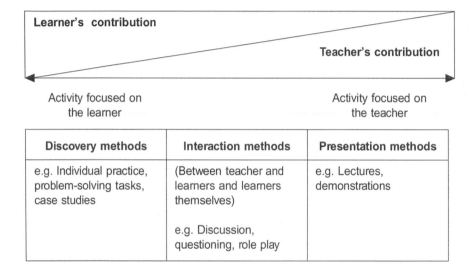

Discovery methods	Interaction methods	Presentation methods
e.g. Individual practice, problem-solving tasks, case studies	(Between teacher and learners and learners themselves) e.g. Discussion, questioning, role play	e.g. Lectures, demonstrations

Figure 3.8 A learner–teacher continuum showing different learning and teaching styles

With these considerations in mind, some of the key principles, discussed in more detail by Truelove (1992), are given below:

- Put teaching and learning into an overarching, contextual picture.
- Give responsibility to the learner.
- Promote variety and interest – by using different methods, groupings, resources.
- Provide an environment conducive to learning.
- Build on the learner's existing knowledge, skills, experience.
- Ensure the learner is actively involved.
- Provide opportunities for constant consolidation and practice.

- Give feedback to the learner as soon as possible and at every opportunity.
- Accentuate the positive achievements of the learner, and build on success.
- Match the pace of learning to suit the individual.
- Promote co-operation among learners – most effective learning usually occurs when collaboration with others takes place.
- Allocate realistic amounts of time for tasks to be completed.
- Encourage high expectations among learners. Expecting learners to do well becomes a self-fulfilling prophecy; when expectations are high all concerned in the learning process make extra efforts and achieve superior outcomes.

TASK SIX

Consider a course you teach. Do you practise the above principles in your teaching? What other key points could be added to the list?

3.6 Monitoring, reviewing and evaluating

In order to ensure that a curriculum is working effectively – namely, that it is relevant to learner needs, the aims and objectives are being achieved, the content is interesting, logical and challenging, teaching and learning methods are inspiring and varied, the assessment methods are measuring the progress of learners and, from a financial viewpoint, value for money is being given – it is essential to carry out a constant process of monitoring, review and evaluation.

The three terms monitoring, review, and evaluation are in practice synonymous, and the purpose of them is to collect information, evidence, criteria and indicators from a diverse range of sources and people in order to analyse what changes can be made to a course to lead to an improvement in its quality and effectiveness. A distinction is made between assessment and evaluation; assessment is the measurement of the progress of the learner, and is considered in Chapter 6, whereas evaluation is a much broader concept which is concerned with considering how successfully all the elements of a curriculum (Figure 3.6) are operating.

The key questions to be asked in any evaluation of a course include the following:

- What is the context and purpose of the evaluation?
- What information, evidence, indicators and criteria can be collected and analysed?
- What methods can be used to collect this information?
- Who should be involved in the evaluation process?
- What problems will occur in the evaluation process?

What is the context and purpose of the evaluation?

In answer to this question, it is useful to consider a framework based on Thomas (1985) which helps to put an evaluation in context by focusing upon the degree of constraint or freedom of the person carrying out the evaluation in choosing the criteria or evidence on the one hand, and in taking part in the preparation of the final evaluation statement or report on the other (see Figure 3.9). When the two axes are placed at right angles to each other, four segments are produced showing four different approaches, as follows:

1. *The professional approach*

This approach enables those being evaluated to set their own evaluative criteria or measures and also play a part in preparing the final evaluative statement. It gives most freedom to those being evaluated, and the main purpose of the evaluation is improvement and development. An example of this approach is teachers' self-evaluation (see section 7.2).

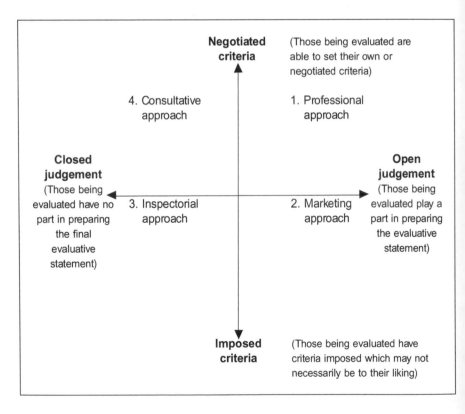

Figure 3.9 Different approaches to curriculum evaluation (based on Thomas, 1985)

2. The marketing approach

In this approach, those being evaluated are not able to set or negotiate the evaluative criteria or measures, but are free to play a part, to a lesser or greater extent, in preparing the final evaluative statement. An example of this is where a college has a set of uniform criteria to be applied to the evaluation of all courses within the college, but where those involved in each course are able to decide the form of the presentation of the evaluation results. There is, therefore, opportunity to present the evaluation results in their best possible light, which could be used, for example, to attract future students and hence market the course.

3. The inspectoral approach

In this segment, those being evaluated have the criteria imposed and do not play any part in preparing the final evaluation statement. An example of this approach is an OFSTED inspection where the evaluation criteria are imposed by OFSTED who have full control over producing the evaluation (inspection) report which is made public.

4. The consultative approach

With this approach those being evaluated are able to set or negotiate the criteria, but not the final evaluative statement. An example of this might be external consultants brought in to evaluate courses within a college, who would negotiate evaluation criteria with those being evaluated, but the latter would have no part in producing the final evaluation report.

These four approaches highlight the different contexts and purposes of evaluation; and also emphasise the importance of relationships between those carrying out the evaluation and those being evaluated. The more involved the latter are in the evaluation process, and the more a sense of 'ownership' of the evaluation is given to them, the less 'threatening' the evaluation process will feel. However, the more 'internal' an evaluation becomes, the more it becomes subjective and biased. Thus any curriculum evaluation has to balance a variety of often conflicting focuses and interests.

Stake (1976) has produced a number of dimensions of evaluation design which highlight the diverse and often conflicting emphases. These are outlined as ends of a continuum with additional notes to clarify each dimension (see Figure 3.10).

What information, evidence, indicators and criteria can be collected and analysed?
What methods can be used to collect this information?
These two questions will be considered together, as evaluative evidence and the methods of obtaining this are very closely interrelated.

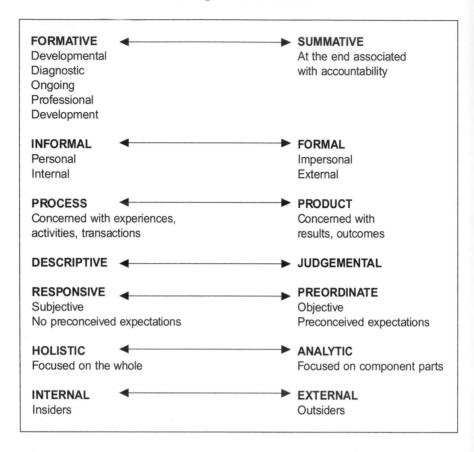

Figure 3.10 Dimensions of curriculum evaluation (based on Stake, 1976)

A helpful way to consider these questions is to classify the various types of evaluative evidence, indicators and criteria into four different categories, namely:

1. survey evidence
2. observational evidence
3. documentary evidence
4. statistical evidence.

As with most classifications, there will necessarily be a degree of overlap between the four types, but it does give us a framework for choosing the most appropriate criteria from the great range available.

1. *Survey evidence*
The main type of evidence in this category is that gained from:

(a) questionnaires
(b) interviews
(c) checklists
(d) discussions.

In each case, evidence is collected from a survey of other people's attitudes and judgements about the course being evaluated.

(a) *Questionnaires*
Their main advantages include:

- speed of collection and analysis of information
- easily administered
- can be anonymous; respondents may be more likely to be truthful.

Some disadvantages might be:

- low response rates if postal questionnaires are used
- misinterpretation of questions by respondents
- in questionnaires where respondents do sign their names, unreliable responses are more likely (for example, the respondent might not want to be seen as being critical of a course or teacher).

Examples of a 'closed' questionnaire and 'open' questionnaire are given in Figures 3.11 and 3.12 respectively. The great advantages of the '**closed**' type of questionnaire are the speed of completion by the respondent, and particularly the ease of processing the responses, especially where these are large in number. The '**open**' questionnaire has the advantage of allowing the respondent to give more comprehensive and original comments but the analysis of free-response comments can be very difficult and time consuming, particularly where a large number of responses has to be considered.

(b) *Interviews*
Have the advantages of:

- probing further into questions than questionnaires
- allowing interviewees to express views in detail.

The disadvantages are:

- the time involved in conducting the interview and in the interpretation of information given
- the great difficulty of preserving anonymity and the consequent problem of the interviewee tending to give responses which he/she thinks the interviewer wants to hear.

PART 1 – On the next four questions, compare this course with others you have taken at this institution, using the following code: 1 = much less than most courses 2 = less than most 3 = about average 4 = more than most 5 = much more than most					
The course: 1. Amount of reading 2. Amount of work in other (non-reading) assignments. 3. Difficulty of subject matter 4. Degree to which the course hung together (various topics and class activities were related to each other).	1 1 1 1	2 2 2 2	3 3 3 3	4 4 4 4	5 5 5 5
PART 2 – Compare the progress you have made in this course with that made in other courses you have taken at this college or university, using the following code: 1 = lowest 10% of courses I have taken here 2 = next 20% 3 = middle 40% 4 = next 20% 5 = upper 10%					
Your progress: 5. Gaining factual knowledge (terminology, classifications, methods trends)	1	2	3	4	5
6. Learning fundamental principles, generalisations or theories 7. Learning to apply course material to improve rational thinking, problem-solving and decision-making	1 1	2 2	3 3	4 4	5 5
8. Developing specific skills, competencies and points of view needed by professionals in the field most closely related to this course	1	2	3	4	5
9. Learning how professionals in this field go about the process of gaining new knowledge	1	2	3	4	5
10. Developing creative capacities 11. Developing a sense of personal responsibility (self-reliance, self-discipline)	1 1	2 2	3 3	4 4	5 5
12. Gaining a broader understanding and appreciation of intellectual cultural activity (music, science, literature, etc.)	1	2	3	4	5
13. Developing skill in expressing myself orally or in writing 14. Discovering the implications of the course material for understanding myself (interests, talents, values etc.)	1 1	2 2	3 3	4 4	5 5
PART 3 – Describe your personal attitudes and behaviour in this course, using the following code: 1 = definitely false 2 = more false than true 3 = in-between 4 = more true than false 5 = definitely true					
Self-rating 15. I worked harder on this course than on most courses I have taken 16. I had a strong desire to take this course 17. I would like to take another class from this instructor 18. As a result of taking this course I have more positive feelings toward this field of study	1 1 1 1	2 2 2 2	3 3 3 3	4 4 4 4	5 5 5 5

PART 4 – The teacher	Excellent		Poor		
19. Variety of teaching methods? 20. Genuine interest in student progress? 21. Preparation for classes? 22. Enthusiasm for subject? 23. Clarity of explanations? 24. Encouragement given to students?	1 1 1 1 1 1	2 2 2 2 2 2	3 3 3 3 3 3	4 4 4 4 4 4	5 5 5 5 5 5

Figure 3.11 An example of a student course evaluation questionnaire with 'closed' questions. (adapted from a questionnaire used at South Carolina State University, USA)

1. What were the most interesting parts of the course?

2. What were the most difficult parts of the course?

3. Which teaching methods did you like best? (Please give your reasons.)

4. In what ways could the course be made more relevant to your job?

5. What other improvements to the course would you recommend?

6. What are your overall impressions of the course?

Figure 3.12. An example of an 'open' questionnaire,
given to learners on a part-time, work-related course

(c) *Checklists*

and

(d) *Discussions* (individual or group)

These are variants of questionnaires and interviews respectively. Checklists can be a very speedy way of gaining feedback on aspects of a course from learners, colleagues etc., while discussions can be a useful interactive way of finding out attitudes about a course. One danger of group discussions is the domination of the group by a few more forceful members, which may distort the representativeness of the group views as a whole.

2. *Observational evidence*

Observation can take place of either learner or teacher activity, or both, to indicate what is happening in the classroom. Two types of scale which are useful in providing a focus are:

(a) 'rating' scales

(b) 'category' systems.

The difference between these is that 'rating' scales indicate the extent to which an observer considers the observed person (e.g. teacher or learner) is achieving various criteria, whereas a 'category' system indicates what is happening in the classroom at every given small time interval, so that by the end of a session an overall picture of an entire teaching session can be determined. There is no particular judgement made on the extent to which criteria are being achieved, or any view that any one particular teaching method is superior to another.

Figures 3.13 and 3.14 show typical rating scales; Figure 3.13 is essentially a rating scale to be completed by learners, and Figure 3.14 to be used by a colleague observing a teaching session.

Figure 3.15 is one of the best known 'category' systems, based on Flanders' Interaction Categories (FIAC) proposed by Flanders (1970). The observer uses the ten categories in conjunction with a grid, each cell of the grid being a ten-second (or some other) time interval. A tick is placed in the appropriate cell every ten seconds throughout the entire teaching session. It is then possible to gain a percentage breakdown of the various activities and interactions taking place in the observed session, which can be useful in comparing the differences in classroom actions and activities of one teacher with different groups, and in comparing the differing classroom activities of different teachers.

Observation of classroom interaction using categories such as that devised by Flanders is a highly skilled activity and needs much practice, but is extremely helpful in determining, without judgemental views, what transactions, activities and experiences are happening in the classroom.

Observational evidence can be collected by a range of different people or 'stakeholders'. These include:

TEACHER RATING QUESTIONNAIRE	Strongly disagree	Disagree	Neither agree nor disagree	Agree	Strongly agree
The lecturer					
Is clear and understandable in his or her explanations	1	2	3	4	5
Stimulates students to think independently	1	2	3	4	5
Makes a genuine effort to get students involved in discussion	1	2	3	4	5
Presents material in a well-organised way	1	2	3	4	5
Makes good use of handouts, e.g. lecture notes, examples of problems, reading lists	1	2	3	4	5
Is sensitive to the feelings and problems of individual students.	1	2	3	4	5
Is enthusiastic about his or her subject	1	2	3	4	5
Stresses important material	1	2	3	4	5
Makes constructive and helpful comments on written work	1	2	3	4	5
Adjusts his or her pace to the needs of the class	1	2	3	4	5
Gives a good factual coverage of the subject matter	1	2	3	4	5
Shows a good sense of humour	1	2	3	4	5
Makes good use of technological aids (e.g. computers, videos)	1	2	3	4	5
Returns written work promptly	1	2	3	4	5
Shows a thorough knowledge of his or her subject	1	2	3	4	5
Shows the relevance of his or her subject to the work you expect to do when you qualify	1	2	3	4	5
Points out the links between his or her subject and related subjects	1	2	3	4	5
Is readily accessible to students outside formal classes	1	2	3	4	5
Encourages students to express their own opinions	1	2	3	4	5
Is always well prepared for his or her classes	1	2	3	4	5
Is punctual and reliable in his or her attendance	1	2	3	4	5
Tries to link lecture material to laboratory work/practical work/fieldwork/seminars	1	2	3	4	5
Can be clearly heard	1	2	3	4	5
States clearly the aims of each session	1	2	3	4	5
Changes his/her approach to meet new situations	1	2	3	4	5

Figure 3.13 A teacher rating scale for use by students (based on a questionnaire used at North East London Polytechnic, now University of East London)

Colleague's name:	Observer:		
Location:	Date/Time:		
Group/Course:	Topic:		
First/Second/Third/Fourth observation	Number of students:		

Planning and preparing work for students	How far achieved?			
	Excellent	Good	Poor	Very poor
1. Appropriate and clearly stated aims and intended outcomes?	1	2	3	4
2. Suitable and interesting subject matter?	1	2	3	4
3. Appropriate teaching and learning strategies?	1	2	3	4
4. Suitable teaching and learning media and resources?	1	2	3	4
5. Appropriate methods for assessing student progress?	1	2	3	4
Teaching and managing				
6. Effective environment?	1	2	3	4
7. Effective introduction?	1	2	3	4
8. Effective development of the session/ activity?	1	2	3	4
9. Effective conclusion of the session/ activity?	1	2	3	4
10. Intentions and outcomes achieved?	1	2	3	4

Further comments on above and overall performance:

Observer:	Date:
Colleague:	Date:

Figure 3.14 An example of a teaching rating scale to be used by a colleague observing a teaching-learning session

		1. *Accepts feeling.* Accepts and clarifies an attitude or the feeling tone of a student in a non-threatening manner. Feelings may be positive or negative. Predicting and recalling feelings are included.
Teacher talk	Response	2. *Praises or encourages.* Praises or encourages student action or behaviour. Jokes that release tension, but not at the expense of another individual; nodding head, or saying 'Um hm?' or 'Go on' are included. 3. *Accepts or uses ideas of students.* Clarifying, building or developing ideas suggested by a student. Teacher extensions of student ideas are included but as the teacher brings more of his/her own ideas into play, shift to category 5.
		4. *Asks questions.* Asking a question about content or procedure, based on teacher ideas, with the intent that a student will answer.
	Initiation	5. *Lecturing.* Giving facts or opinions about content or procedures; expressing his/her own ideas, giving his/her own explanation, or citing an authority other than the student. 6. *Giving directions.* Directions, commands or orders which a student is expected to comply. 7. *Criticising or justifying authority.* Statements intended to change student behaviour from non-acceptable to acceptable pattern; bawling someone out; stating why the teacher is doing what he/she is doing; extreme self-reference.
Student talk	Response	8. *Student talk – response.* Talk by students in response to teacher. Teacher initiates the contact or solicits student statement or structures the situation. Freedom to express own ideas is limited.
	Initiation	9. *Student talk – initiation.* Talk by students which they initiate. Expressing own ideas; initiating a new topic; freedom to develop opinions and a line of thought, like asking thoughtful questions going beyond the existing structure.
Silence		10. *Silence or confusion.* Pauses, short periods of silence and periods of confusion in which communication cannot be understood by the observer.

Figure 3.15 An interaction category system (based on Flanders, 1970)

- the teacher himself/herself
- a colleague
- the learners
- an external observer.

As evaluation can be such a subjective and biased activity, it is helpful to obtain observational evidence from a variety of different types of observers, each with a different perspective.

In addition to, or instead of, direct observation by the 'stakeholders' noted above, observational evidence can be collected by:

- video recording
- audio recording
- photography.

Each of these, particularly video recording, offers a powerful way of analysing and evaluating a teaching session after it has finished, either privately or in conjunction with other 'stakeholders'.

3. *Documentary evidence*
The main types of documentary evidence are:

- minutes of course meetings or staff–student meetings
- syllabi
- schemes of work and teaching plans
- reports from inspectors, advisers, moderators
- textbooks and other recommended publications
- coursework, and course notes made by learners
- timetables
- diaries
- letters
- memos.

The above can show different dimensions of a course, and different viewpoints. Diaries, for example, can be kept by teachers or learners to record observations, reflections, feelings, anxieties, reactions etc., either systematically or in a more open-ended, impressionistic way. Minutes of staff–student meetings can reveal clearly the key issues, both positive and negative, about a course. In addition, the contributors to meetings can indicate the different stances and emphases that exist within a course team and in the interaction between teachers and learners.

4. *Statistical evidence*
There is a very wide range of statistical evidence, information or indicators available

which may be helpful in course evaluation, including:

- examination, test results, and results from other forms of assessment
- student retention/completion rates
- attendance and punctuality rates
- teacher/learner ratios
- entry qualifications of the learners
- other characteristics of the learners; for example, age, gender, nationality, part-time or full-time
- learner destination information; for example, what proportion of learners progress to other courses, the types of employment learners proceed to, the proportions of learners unemployed six months after completion of the course
- the cost of the course, especially relative to the cost of other courses, and other financial indicators
- time aspects of courses; for example, the time per week or per year spent on actual teaching (class contact time); the time spent by teachers on assessing; the time learners spend on producing assignments; the time learners spend on work placements, work experience.

Statistical evidence has many advantages, viz.:

- it is relatively easy and speedy to collect
- it tends to be more objective and less liable to bias than some other types of evidence
- it often offers opportunity for comparison and contrast which can be extremely beneficial and salutary for both teachers and learners. For example, examination pass rates from a range of courses can be easily shown, which can indicate and inform about aspects of those courses.

TASK SEVEN

Think of the course(s) you are involved with. Within each of the four main types outlined above – (1) survey, (2) observational, (3) documentary, (4) statistical – identify other items which would be useful in evaluating your course(s).

Who should be involved in the evaluation process?

It is useful to gather a wide range of evidence, information, opinion and measures when evaluating, and ideally this should involve all those directly and indirectly connected with the course, often known as 'the stakeholders'. Course evaluation might therefore include the following:

- the teacher(s) directly involved in teaching
- the learner(s) directly involved with the course
- previous learners
- potential future learners
- teachers, colleagues not involved in teaching the course
- employers who might be involved through work-placement, work-experience schemes
- parents (of younger learners, especially those just entering further education)
- governors (of educational organisations)
- representatives of the media, who can be very helpful in highlighting beneficial aspects of course, but can also distort negative evaluation results which are made public!

What problems will occur in the evaluation process?

There are many problems associated with evaluation: some can be prevented or alleviated with prior care; some are an integral part of the evaluative process. The main problems are outlined below:

- Evaluation can be extremely time consuming. Unless care is taken it can take up a disproportionate amount of time and energy.

- It can be negative, threatening and destructive. There may be a tendency for various 'stakeholders' to focus on the shortcomings of a course, rather than the more positive aspects.

- For the teacher, the fear and reality of negative results may be threatening and have a deleterious effect on teaching and learning and wider issues involving the teacher–learner relationship.

- Evaluation results can be biased. It is therefore important to include a diverse range of evidence from different sources and stakeholders to try to eliminate such bias and distortion. Even when this is done, bias can occur, as sometimes, for example in interviews, respondents give the answer they think the interviewer wants to hear, rather than the 'real' or truthful response.

- It can sometimes be difficult or impossible to introduce some of the changes recommended in a course evaluation. Therefore, the stakeholders involved in such an evaluation might become disillusioned and see little point in taking part in further evaluations. For example, an evaluation may reveal that the room used for a course is too small, or badly shaped, or has furniture which is uncomfortable. These shortcomings may be out of the control of the individual teacher, and thus it may be impossible to act, at least in the short term, upon results of an evaluation.

TASK EIGHT

Identify some of the other problems you might anticipate in evaluating one of your courses.

Think of the ways in which these problems can be minimised.

3.7 Curriculum innovation

As a result of evaluation, it is often found that some sort of change or innovation is necessary or desirable in a course. A distinction is sometimes made between the terms 'change' and 'innovation', the latter being defined as a deliberate and planned change, whereas the former may be unplanned and haphazard.

Types of innovation

There are many types but the clearest way of approaching innovation is to think of two major emphases at each end of a continuum (see Figure 3.16). In forced or imposed innovation, there is the danger of resentment and hostility among the people having to carry out the innovation, which is imposed with little or no consultation.

Voluntary innovation, on the other hand, emphasises that the 'change agents' (the promoters of the innovation) deliberately try to involve as many of those involved in the innovation as possible, through discussion, consultation, co-operation, collaboration etc. Therefore this approach to innovation can be very slow since it often involves changing attitudes and values, but can be more successful than forced innovation in the long run, as all involved feel they have had a say in the planning and introduction of the innovation.

Forced, imposed, innovation ('Top down'.) innovation. Often has the power of a legislating body to introduce change. Little discussion or consultation. Can be speedy.	Various hybrid types exist at various points along the continuum	Voluntary innovation. ('Bottom up'.) Starts with the need to solve a practical problem, as seen by teachers or learners. Much discussion and consultation at every stage Can be very slow moving.

Figure 3.16 Types of innovation

Attitudes to innovation

After studying different innovations over many years, Rogers and Shoemaker (1971) developed a continuum of dispositions towards innovation, which has been further refined by Pratt (1980) (see Figure 3.17). It is a generalised idea, and there could, of course, be differences in the proportions of the attitudes shown in Figure 3.17 depending on many factors, including the way the innovation is introduced, namely forced or voluntary, the type of innovation, the size and context of the organisation where the innovation is introduced etc.

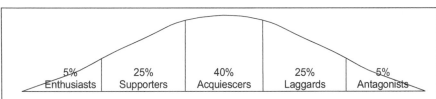

The *enthusiasts* are characterised by vigour and independence of outlook. They need adventure, enjoy making changes and taking risks, and have high aspirations. They are gregarious and are likely to have contact with other change agents and sources of information from outside the organisation. The enthusiasts are likely to participate in the design or testing of the innovation.

The *supporters* are respected members of the organization, who have a less radical image than the enthusiasts. Like the enthusiasts, they tend to be actively involved in professional associations and in-service training. They are knowledgeable about curriculum issues and are quickly persuaded of the value of an innovation once it has been thoroughly planned, justified and tested.

The *acquiescers* are phlegmatic and deliberate in their approach to change. While prepared to consider change, they will not initiate it. Most of their contacts are with their peers within the organisation. They tend to take the line of least resistance and hence will adopt a change, at least superficially, as soon as opposition becomes onerous.

The *laggards* tend to have a low profile in the organisation and have few contacts outside their peer group. They are characteristically sceptical about changes. They tend to be dogmatic and fatalistic and have difficulty dealing with abstractions. They are fixed in a certain way of life and will not change until the majority of colleagues have done so.

The *antagonists* are loners. They resist changes for deep-seated psychological or philosophical reasons. They may work actively or passively to sabotage innovations that are proposed or introduced.

Figure 3.17. Attitudes towards innovation (based on Pratt, 1980)

The continuum of attitudes is particularly helpful in making us aware of the resistance which may be encountered towards innovation and in explaining why the process of innovation can be so slow.

Stages of innovation

Usually an innovation goes through a number of distinct steps along a continuum, shown in Figure 3.18. Although shown as a linear progression, the route from creation to institutionalisation can be full of twists and turns, and the initial innovation may even be modified and reformed before further progress is possible.

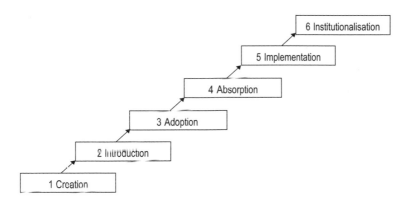

Figure. 3.18 Stages of Innovation

TASK NINE

Consider any curriculum innovations which have taken place in your organisation recently. Have the innovations been forced or voluntary?

Which colleagues have displayed the attitudes outlined in Figure 3.17?

In which attitude category would you place yourself?

Which factors most influence your innovation attitude?

Summary

In this chapter, many aspects of curriculum design and evaluation have been considered. You should now have a better understanding of the following areas:

- the key elements which make up a curriculum
- four different models of curriculum planning
- the characteristics of the 'hidden' curriculum
- three different educational ideologies which can provide a source of objectives
- some important principles of selecting content and choosing teaching and learning methods
- techniques and evidence for curriculum evaluation
- different types of curriculum innovation, attitudes towards innovation, and stages in the process of innovation.

The curriculum is a very large area of focus, rather like a huge jigsaw, made up of many parts. It must always be remembered that the learner is of utmost importance in curriculum planning. Any decision made in curriculum design and evaluation must bear in mind the key question: 'In what ways will the learner benefit from this?'

References and further reading

Apple, M.W. (1979) *Ideology and Curriculum*. London: Routledge and Kegan Paul.

Ausubel, D.P. and Robinson, F.G. (1969) *School Learning: an Introduction to Educational Psychology*. New York: Holt, Rinehart and Winston.

Bloom, B.S. (ed.) (1956) *Taxonomy of Educational Objectives, Handbook I: Cognitive Domain*. New York: David McKay.

Bloom, B. S. and Krathwell, D. R. (1954) *A Taxomony of Educational Objectives, Handbook 1, The Cognitive Process*. New York: David McKay.

Bobbitt, F. (1918) *The Curriculum*. Boston: Houghton Mifflin.

Bobbitt, F. (1924) *How to Make a Curriculum*. Boston: Houghton Mifflin.

Bruner, J.S. (1960) *The Process of Education*. Cambridge, MA., Harvard University Press.

Dressel, P.L. (1982) 'Curriculum and instruction in higher education' in Mitzel. H.E. (ed.) *Encyclopedia of Educational Research*. Englewood Cliffs, NJ: The Free Press.

Ebel, R.L. (1972) *Essentials of Educational Measurements*. New York: Prentice Hall.

Farrell, M. Kerry, T. and Kerry, C. (1995) *The Blackwell Handbook of Education*. Oxford: Blackwell.

Flanders, N. A. (1970) *Analyzing Teaching Behaviour*. Reading, MA. Addison-Wesley.

Gagné, R.M. (1975) *The Conditions of Learning*. New York: Holt, Rinehart and Winston.

Golby, M. (1977) 'Curriculum studies and education for teaching', *Journal of Further and Higher Education.* Vol. 1, no. 1, pp. 68–77.

Hamilton, D. et al. (1976) *Beyond the Numbers Game.* London: Macmillan

Hirst, P. H. (1974) *Knowledge and The Curriculum.* London: Routledge and Kegan Paul.

Hughes, M., Ribbins, P. and Thomas, H. (eds). (1985) *Managing Education: The System and the Institution.* London: Holt.

Jenkins, D. and Shipman, M. D. (1976) *Curriculum: An Introduction.* London: Open Books.

Kelly, A.V. (1987) *Education.* London: Heinemann.

Kerr, J. F. (ed.) (1968) *Changing the Curriculum.* London: University of London Press.

Krathwohl, D.R., Bloom, B.S. and Maria, B.B. (1964) *A Taxonomy of Educational Objectives, Handbook 2, The Affective Doman.* New York: David McKay.

Lawton, D. (1983) *Curriculum Studies and Educational Planning.* London: Hodder and Stoughton.

Macdonald-Ross, M. (1973) Behavioural objectives: a critical review, *Instructional Science*, Vol. 2.

Peters, R. S. (1966) *Ethids and Education.* London: Allen and Unwin.

Pratt, D. (1980) *Curriculum: Design and Development.* New York: Harcourt Brace Jovanovich.

Richmond, W.K. (1971) *The School Curriculum.* London: Methuen.

Rogers, A. (1986) *Teaching Adults.* Milton Keynes: Open University Press.

Rogers, E.M. and Shoemaker, F. (1971) *Communication of Innovation.* New York: The Free Press.

Scrimshaw, P. (1983) *Purpose and Planning in the Curriculum.* Second Level Course, E204, Unit 2, Educational Ideologies. Milton Keynes: Open University Press.

Skilbeck, M. (1976) *Ideology, Knowledge and the Curriculum.* Milton Keynes: Open University Press.

Snyder, B.R. (1971) *The Hidden Curriculum.* New York: Alfred A. Knopf.

Sockett, H. (1976) *Designing the Curriculum.* London: Open Books.

Stake, R.E. (1976) *Evaluating Educational Programmes.* Paris: OECD.

Stenhouse, L. (1975) *An Introduction to Curriculum Research and Development.* London: Heinemann.

Taba, H. (1962) *Curriculum Development: Theory and Practice.* New York: Harcourt, Brace and World.

Thomas, H. (1985) 'Perspectives on evaluation', in Hughes, M. et al. (eds) *Managing Education: The System and the Institution. London: Holt.*

Truelove, S. (ed.) (1992) *The Handbook of Training and Development.* Oxford: Blackwell.

Tyler, R.W. (1949) *Basic Principles of Curriculum and Instruction.* Chicago: University of Chicago Press.

Wheeler, D. K. (1967) *Curriclum Process.* London: University of London Press.

4

Planning Your Teaching

CHAPTER OUTLINE

Careful planning is a key feature of successful teaching and learning. The more experience you gain, the more your planning will become internalised and you will automatically select the best methods and organisation. However, in the early stages of your teaching career, or with a new group or a new course, you should carefully think through the stages of the session to select the most efficient teaching and learning methods. This chapter considers some of the factors you should take into account in such planning. It justifies the effects of good planning (4.1) and looks at the different time frames you should plan within as well as examining the two dimensions of the content and the learners (4.3). Defining specific and appropriate learning purposes in the light of all these dimensions is an essential skill (4.4). You can then proceed to select the appropriate teaching methods (4.5). You may not be able to choose where you will teach but you can make the most of that environment (4.7). Finally, what will be your role? How will you use your learners' responses to adapt your own style and assess if they have learned? (4.6) (4.8)

Careful planning is the key to successful sessions and courses. Many experienced teachers plan in their heads but more and more organisations, acknowledging the effect of planning on the quality of student learning, are requiring teachers to submit short-term and medium-term planning to line managers.

The old saying 'fail to plan and plan to fail' may sound rather pessimistic but is often true. Even the most experienced teachers have had sessions where they have lost track and the session has wandered off course.

A plan gives you a structured format within which you can be confident that you are meeting learners' needs.

The FENTO Standards addressed in this chapter

Many aspects of Key Area B – Planning your teaching – are addressed in this chapter. For example:

B1 Identify the required outcomes of the learning programme

(b) produce learning outcomes from programmes of study

B2 Identify the appropriate teaching and learning techniques

(b) select appropriate teaching techniques to accommodate different styles of learning

c) use individual, small-group and whole-group teaching techniques as appropriate

d) set precise targets with individual learners

This chapter also gives some generic knowledge of the following:

• ways of selecting teaching methods
• what is involved in individual and group learning (also addressed in Chapter 5).

4.1 Why plan?

To gain confidence
Planning gives you the confidence to know where you are going in a session. There are many things in teaching which you may have less control over, the room, the number of learners, the time given to particular topics etc., meaning that it is essential to have a planned progression for the session so that you and the learners are clear about your intentions. During a session you may have to make many split-second judgements about, for example, how to respond to behaviour, how to rephrase explanations, how to frame an effective question to learners. A plan allows you to get back on course and successfully achieve your learning outcomes. Of course, plans have to respond to the learners' needs and may have to be revised after particular sessions, but the planning framework should allow you to have the confidence to be flexible while ensuring the learners obtain the training to which they are entitled.

To ensure coverage of curriculum
The vast majority of courses in post-16 education and training have a time requirement for finalisation and criteria for successful completion. This means that decisions have to be taken about such factors as the time taken on particular topics, which concepts are essential to further understanding and which are likely to be less

important. Effective plans will ensure that the time spent at different phases of the course will be appropriate to the syllabus and the learners. It is no good spending a disproportionate length of time on what may be a very fascinating subject if there is then little time to devote to other essential aspects which will be assessed.

There should also be continuity within the course. Skills, concepts and knowledge should build up in a logical manner to ensure that learners progress smoothly. Learning is most effective if it relates clearly to existing knowledge, and links should be made explicitly, as well as being implicit in the programme.

To ensure consistency

There will probably be a team of teachers working on one particular course and there may well be more than one group studying the same course. It is therefore important to ensure that the experience for all learners is the same. Detailed planning is the key to achieving this although even the most rigorous plans cannot ensure uniformity across a range of teacher styles and preferences. When a teacher teaches the same material to different groups it quickly becomes clear how much the teacher is influenced by the learners. Different groups naturally evolve their own character and the teacher responds to that in the way s/he teaches. However, learners are entitled to access to the full curriculum and within the course team the plans should clearly show consistency and continuity so that each teacher is confident that their input fits perfectly into the whole.

To ensure balance in the course and in the structure of sessions

We have already discussed the wide variety of learning styles there will be within your classes (see 2.5). In order to maintain learners' concentration and motivation for perhaps 2–3 hours and over a period of time it is essential to vary the demands placed upon them. The concept of fitness for purpose, i.e. matching the teaching strategy to the learning outcome required, is discussed later in this chapter but there should also be changes in student activity during and across sessions. Planning a group of sessions (see Medium-term plans) will ensure that there is an overall balance between teaching and learning strategies, new knowledge and revision, variation in learner activity and breadth and balance of the curriculum.

4.2 Dimensions of planning

Timephase

Long term
A long-term outline plan probably conforms to a great extent to the syllabus provided. It will lay out the learning outcomes in terms of the assessment. Sometimes it is defined by units and it is usually prescriptive in its layout.

Medium term
Medium-term plans can be useful in further defining content against learning outcomes on a session-by-session basis.

More detail can be added here to relate the kinds and stages of assessment to the curriculum and also a brief indication of teaching strategy to be used. A well-defined medium-term plan ensures the progression and balance of a series of teaching sessions as well as ensuring progression and continuity.

Short term
An individual plan is used for each session. It should have clear learning purposes to sharpen the focus and show the progression of the session as well as indicating how learners will be assessed. A session plan is most effective when a brief outline is shared with learners. The more learners know about what will be presented to them the easier it is to follow the session.

Many organisations have their own session plan format. They all tend to cover the same areas and it is up to individual teachers to choose a layout which best fits their purpose. The areas are:

- learning purpose/learning objectives/learning outcomes
- an estimate of how long each part of the session will take
- what learners will do
- what the teacher will do
- what questions may be asked
- how learners will be assessed
- resources required.

Planning considerations
At each level of planning the two dimensions to be considered are the **learners** and the nature and content of the **curriculum**. Figure 4.1 includes some of the questions you may need to answer in relation to each of those dimensions.

4.3 Planning to meet learner needs
New teachers are naturally concerned primarily with the subject content they are to teach. After all, their expertise in their subject is the reason for their appointment. However, we have all experienced a lecture or TV programme or text which, although excellent in its own right, has been so far removed from our own experience that it has failed to stimulate us and we have eventually given up trying to understand it. The learners and their needs must be considered for successful learning. Below are some of the issues to be addressed when considering learners' previous learning history.

Age/maturity
Learners bring to new learning their own experiences and perceptions of themselves

	Learners	Curriculum
Long term	• What is the learners' previous experience as learners? In relation to the course material? • Do learners understand the rationale for the course?	• What are the learning outcomes of the course? • How will the course be assessed? • How does the material relate to the needs of the sector? Employability? • What flexibility is there within the syllabus?
Medium term	• Is sufficient time given to revision and consolidation of learning? • Is the time spent on each new topic consistent? • Is the material presented in such a way as to relate to the course aims? • Are learners always clear as to the purpose of current study topics? • Will these topics motivate the learners?	• Is there a balance of material over the course? • What is the proportion of time spent on assessment in relation to new material? • Do the study topics offer a progression in learning? • Which are the topics that the learners will have most difficulty with?
Short term	• What time is available? • Which teaching room is to be used, and what is the best seating arrangement for this session? • Do the learners have the necessary skills for this kind of learning, e.g. group work, library research skills? • Size of group?	• Are the teaching methods congruent with the material? • What are the learning outcomes for this session? • How good is your subject knowledge in this area?

Figure 4.1 Planning considerations

as learners. Some learners enter further education having failed to a great extent in schools. Other mature learners may not have been in education for some time and have outdated images of what 'education' is like. You may have many different kinds of learners within the group. It is useful to begin a period of study with some discussion about what learners' perceptions are of the course and of themselves and to further explore this in tutorials. Learners are not just 'empty vessels' into which you must pour knowledge. In order for them to learn they must engage with the course and actively involve themselves. As the teacher it is your responsibility actively to involve all of them.

Motivation

Learners embark on a course for a variety of reasons. For some learners the outcome of your course may be a passport to future prospects. For other learners there may, at this stage, be no apparent reason for the training. They may not have had a particular choice and may have been sent by, perhaps, family, DSS, line managers etc. Learners' individual reasons will affect their motivation, i.e. how positive they feel about it. This in turn will affect their behaviour in the class and the strategies you should use to enable them to learn.

Concentration span

The ability to concentrate for long periods of time is a learned skill. Learners' concentration levels will vary according to how much study they have undertaken recently and their different levels of study skills. Thus, when starting to study a new subject, learners need course material which is presented in a variety of ways and individual sessions should be planned with this in mind. Reading should also be carefully chosen so that learners can relate at their own level. As the course progresses, so the length of concentration period can increase. Learners will by then have gained the necessary study skills to enable them to concentrate for longer.

Stage in the programme

We have already discussed how learners' concentration should improve over the course of study and how you should plan for this in your short- and medium-term plans. Learners at the beginning of a course may be anxious and apprehensive. They want to know that they will be able to succeed and the messages you send out by the work planned at that stage will either confirm or allay their anxieties. For example, if the early sessions demand too much of learners, they may lose confidence in their own ability as well as possibly missing out on valuable foundation content. At the beginning of a course, learners are also getting used to you and each other so that not all their energies are necessarily going into the learning process. Much of their time and effort is spent trying to determine what is required of them by the course, their fellow learners and, most importantly to them, you.

How are they used to studying?
We have discussed learning styles and learners' own preferred learning styles (see Section 2.5). There is also another factor which makes up their history as learners – the preferred teaching style of their former teachers. It is therefore important to make explicit your own preferences at the beginning of a session – do you expect them to take notes in every session? Will you give copies of your OHTs at the end of the session? Can learners ask questions at any time? Do you prefer them to wait until an appropriate time? Do you expect silence? A quiet room? Even the most basic of issues such as what they should call you should be made clear at the outset to avoid confusion and enable every student to feel confident in their responses to the learning situation.

Ability
There may be entry criteria to the course on which you teach but those criteria may only give you a rough range of abilities within which your learners fit. There is also a limit to what that information can tell you about your learners. For example, although a GCSE Grade C in English may indicate a certain overall standard, it may not indicate a student's verbal ability or the ability to understand a certain vocabulary. It may not offer any insights into which learners are slow to learn new material or lacking in confidence in certain areas. All these other factors are what makes learners individuals. It is easy to pretend that all learners are starting from the same position on the blocks but that is not usually the case.

Prior knowledge
Your learners will come to your course with a range of existing knowledge in relation to the course material. Thus, some may have had employment in related areas while others may have qualifications related to theoretical aspects of the subject. Some of your learners' existing knowledge may be partial, some may be wrong. Current theories of learning acknowledge that learning builds upon a 'scaffold' of existing experiences. You need to establish the structure of your learners' existing scaffold and it may subsequently be necessary to revise or review.

Confidence
In the above paragraphs we have talked a lot about confidence. No one learns effectively if they are anxious or unsure. It is your task, as a teacher, to make clear your expectations of the learning situation so that learners are clear about what is expected of them and what they can expect from you. It is this that gives us confidence in new situations that we will not 'get things wrong' or be 'made a fool of'. You should bear all these factors in mind when you are planning both individual sessions and the whole course. Of course, you cannot cater for every individual at every stage but broadly speaking you should try to address some of these factors in order that your learners should learn. The aim of education is not only for you to

teach but for your learners to learn and if various factors inhibit learning, strategies should be developed to minimise them. In the next chapter self-esteem is discussed together with the need for teachers to build a positive learning environment.

4.4 Defining learning purposes

The single most important thing a teacher needs to do to ensure effective teaching and learning is to define specifically what the learners should know, whether by the end of a course, or by the end of the session. If the teacher is unclear then teaching will be unfocused and the learners will therefore be unsure about what they are supposed to be learning.

Do you want to teach your learners a **skill** or some **knowledge** or a **concept** (see **Task One**)?

TASK ONE

Consider the learning purposes below and place them in the categories given. Then consider how specific they are. Once defined, you should be able to know after the session whether the learners have learned it.

Learners should:

1. become familiar with the organisation's appraisal policy
2. know the elements of a successful meeting
3. understand how to measure viscosity
4. be able to use a particular desktop publishing package
5. be familiar with the new Criminal Act
6. know how to do long division
7. understand the role of a Primary Health Team
8. know how children learn to read

Concept	Knowledge	Skill

In defining your learning purpose you should consider whether it is viable within the time available and the learners you have. Does it relate to past sessions and if so do you make the links clear? Does it build on past learning and in turn lay foundations for future work? Can learners see its relevance to the syllabus and the qualification? Because of all these issues you should try to map out learning purposes of individual sessions at the medium-term planning stage to ensure progression.

Once you have identified clear learning purposes you should share them with the group so that learners are in the appropriate mind-set. The more they know about the structure of the session the more they can make links themselves and follow the progression.

4.5 Teaching strategies: matching method to purpose

Once you have defined the learning purpose, the appropriate teaching and learning strategies should be matched to them.

For example, if learners are learning a skill, they may need initially to watch a demonstration before practising individually or in groups. It will not be appropriate for them to be told what to do. You should use what you know about how learners learn to choose the appropriate method. Will it be appropriate for students to work together, in which case group work may be an option?

Is this learning new for them or are they practising what has already been introduced? This clearly has implications for the time you spend on particular activities. If you intend to introduce new material you should give time for questions and explanations and possibly reiterate the same thing in different ways. You should also be aware that this will require greater concentration from learners and you may need to balance the session with some less demanding material at some stage. You should also be conscious that you will have to build some time (however short) into the next session to revise and check on learning.

4.6 Planning for the role of the teacher

When planning for learning, it is obvious that you should plan for what the learners will be doing. In following that through you should get an idea of what the experience will be like for the learner – how manageable it is, how balanced the session is, whether the expectations placed on the learner are reasonable. However, you should also consider your own role. Are there opportunities for you to fulfil a number of tasks within a session? Can you check on learning through questions? Can you give individual help for those who are likely to have difficulties assimilating new knowledge? Can you circulate around the classroom to ensure that learners remain on task or to intervene and teach individuals or small groups? You may wish to give learners activities at some point which they can get on with independently to leave you free to perform any of these tasks. You should try not to wander around the room aimlessly, 'creating a draught' or conversely in fire fighting mode, flapping away at several different activities, but ensure that you have already identified when, where and how you are likely to be deployed.

4.7 The learning environment

Few teachers have the luxury of having a room allocated solely to them and/or for their subject. For most it is a case of making the best of what is timetabled. It is important to match the room as far as possible to the needs of the group and the session. This may well mean that you have to change the layout of the room, sometimes without being able to enter before the session begins. If you set up the expectation that tables may be moved, it becomes a habit. The following is a checklist to help you to address important factors:

- Can you see everywhere in the classroom?
- Can you easily access all areas?
- Can learners see the teaching aids you will use, e.g. OHP, board, VCR?
- Does the layout of the room allow learners to focus upon you or upon each other, depending on which teaching strategy you are using?
- Does the layout allow learners enough room to move?
- Is there sufficient ventilation at all stages of the session?

It is important to remember to vary your own position in the room. When you are at the front you have a very limited range – the focus is forward and middle distance. By changing position you can give greater attention to all learners, even those who deliberately sit at the back.

Obviously, the more attractive the environment, the more conducive to learning. Again, if you set expectations that the room will be tidy and clear of litter etc. before the sessions start, you establish a habit.

4.8 Planning for assessment

Assessment is the way in which teachers find out if learning has taken place. It can occur formally or informally throughout a session. The feedback a teacher receives from the learners will enable him/her to make decisions about whether to move on to the next point of the session or slow the pace down or explain something in another way. Thus the teacher 'reads' the group and responds accordingly. Although these assessments may be informal, and include strategies such as questioning, they are an important source of feedback and should be considered at the point of planning. Assessment is an integral part of the teaching/learning process and is addressed comprehensively in Chapter 6. You should remember, however, to build it into your plans for individual sessions and courses.

Summary

If the key to successful teaching is planning then the key to successful planning is the ability of the teacher to consider the requirements of both the learners and the course. This chapter has looked at planning across different dimensions and has given you a framework within which short-term learning processes are identified and the appropriate teaching strategies matched to them.

In considering the learner, you should now be able to identify the important characteristics which relate not only to ability but also to attitudes, stages of the course, confidence etc. Matching the learning to the learner is both complex and vital in successful teaching and learning.

References and further reading

General
FENTO (1999) *Standards for Teaching and Supporting Learning in Further Education in England and Wales.* London: FENTO.

Planning your teaching
Gibbs, G. and Habeshaw, T. (1992) 3rd edn. *253 Ideas for Your Teaching.* Bristol: Technical and Educational Services.
Reynolds, M. (1994) *Group Work in Education and Training.* London: Kogan Page.
Rogers, A. (1996) *Teaching Adults,* Milton Keynes: Open University Press.

5

Managing Learning

CHAPTER OUTLINE

In managing the sessions you teach there are a number of underlying principles which should shape the actions you, the teacher, takes. This chapter addresses these issues. It considers your own role when managing a group (5. 1). It also considers strategies for you to implement in managing your learners' behaviour, using a model which analyses these strategies into preventative, corrective and those which build and develop positive learner/teacher relationships (5.3). As a teacher, you must recognise how your learners learn and why they want to learn. What motivates them and how you can encourage them to bring a positive approach to the learning process. These issues are addressed in 5.2. The role of language in clearly organising and conveying your material is important and the skill of giving an effective explanation is considered in 5.4. Finally in this chapter, the whole concept of Inclusive Education and Training is briefly considered. Teachers, in further education organisations in particular, will need to read more about this and you should receive support from your own staff development departments to begin to implement some of the principles. The concept of Inclusive Education and Training emphasises that good practice adheres to the same principles for all learners, thus providing equality of opportunity for all.

The FENTO Standards addressed in this chapter

Many aspects of Key Area D – Managing the learning process are addressed in this chapter. For example:

D1 Establish and maintain an effective learning environment

D2 Plan and structure learning activities

(f) use a variety of teaching methods to meet the needs of groups and individuals and to provide an environment in which all learners have the opportunity to experience success

D3 Communicate effectively with learners

(b) present information to learners clearly and in an appropriate format

In addition the standards in B2 – Identify appropriate teaching and learning techniques – are also addressed in this chapter:

B2 (c) use individual, small-group and whole-group teaching techniques as appropriate

B2 (e) create a safe learning environment based on trust and support

B2 (d) support a culture of open access and widening participation

5.1 Managing large and small groups

During any course or individual session, your learners will be working either individually, in small groups or pairs, or as a whole group.

The concept of **fitness for purpose** has been introduced in Chapter 4, that is, the need to fit the teaching and learning strategy to the learning purpose. Thus it is important first to define what you want your learners to learn and then to decide the most appropriate way for them to learn, either collaboratively in small groups or individually or as a whole group. In each of these scenarios it is important to consider your own role in managing learning.

Managing the whole group

Whole-group teaching may occur at some points in any sessions or there may be times when you need to give the same information or introduction for the majority of a session. In your planning you should give consideration to the level of material you use and the ways in which you will ensure that your learners engage with that material so that the session remains as interactive as possible. During the session you should remain sensitive to your learners and focus on them as well as the material you are offering. In monitoring a whole-group session you should adopt strategies to allow you to:

- ensure that you have the attention of the whole group before you begin.
- clearly frame the learning purpose and explain the relevance of the material you are about to teach
- use resources and teaching aids (e.g. wipe board, overhead projector) to enable a multi-sensory approach
- ensure that all learners understand at each point in the session
- change your position in the room to ensure that you can view all learners and use your own presence and proximity to bring all learners back on task
- make clear at the beginning of the session the role of the learner: should they take notes, actively use a handout or *aide-memoir* etc.
- use questioning to maintain interest and attention as well as to check understanding
- vary your voice and the pace of the session to maintain the learners' interest
- regularly scan the learners to ensure that they are all on task
- interpret non-verbal cues to ascertain whether learners are still concentrating.

Managing small groups

Discussion is an important part of the learning process. Learners must have the opportunity to discuss, problem-solve, dispute, share experience and collaborate in groups. Group work, however, needs careful planning and managing to ensure that all learners engage with the exercise and fulfil the intended learning outcomes. If you choose to use this method regularly you should enhance your own skills and expertise by studying the subject further. Some references for this are given at the end of this chapter.

There are many different kinds of group work. Sometimes learners are engaged in individual work which has a joint outcome. Collaborative group work requires learners to be dependent on each other to fulfil the task. Your first task in planning is to decide what you want your learners to learn and thus which kind of group work is appropriate to the learning experience. On a basic level these are some of the issues you should consider:

The correct grouping for the task

In making your decision about grouping you should consider how best your learners work, what the demands of the tasks are and how you will use the personalities within the group. How can you frame the task to ensure that quieter members of the group are not dominated by more confident learners?

There are a number of ways in which to group learners:

- friendship groups
- groups of similar ability or experience
- groups of similar age (usually the distinction is between mature learners and younger ones)
- groups of mixed age or experience or ability.

A word of warning! Classrooms are sometimes arranged in groups of tables so that learners are automatically seated in groups. These ad hoc groups are not always appropriate for some kinds of collaborative group work and you may well have to make some changes. However, people do not always like to be moved once settled so if you intend to make any changes to seating arrangements, try to do so before the beginning of the session and make it clear early in the course that this will happen.

Working collaboratively
Teachers often assume that adult learners already have the skills to work collaboratively. This is not so: many adults lack these skills and have to learn to work together just as they have to learn other things. Before embarking on group work you should discuss with your learners the skills involved in working in groups. The following is a list of the rules of group work generated by a group of adults recently.

Group members should:

• listen to each other
• let one person speak at a time
• let every person have their say
• all contribute
• not laugh at anyone
• resolve disagreements by discussion, and ultimately by a vote.

In a plenary you should give learners the opportunity to reflect on how they have performed both individually and as a group.

Structuring group work
It is important for your learners to be clear about the purpose of the group work activity and what the outcome should be. Thus the task should be tightly structured, particularly if your learners are not used to working in groups. In introducing the work you should inform your learners about:

• the purpose of the task
• the outcome
• the time they have to complete it
• the support they can expect from you
• the resources they can use
• how it will be assessed
• the importance of collaboration.

It is important to allow time before the end of the session for feedback on the group's outcomes. This may be formative if the task is to last for more than one session but is none the less essential to reinforce the accountability of the groups. If the task is to last for several sessions it is important to structure it so that the groups do not lose track of what they are doing, nor lose the momentum.

TASK ONE

Draft out a group-work activity you might use on one of your courses. Using the framework above, plan the introductory instructions you would give to the groups.

Monitoring group work

As well as carefully structuring the task, you should consider your own role in the group's learning. Will you be:

- **A fire-fighter**: moving from group to group as problems occur?

- **A teacher**: moving from group to group, posing questions, suggesting resources etc.?

- **An encourager**: maintaining the momentum when groups wander off the track?

- **A counsellor**: guiding learners in how to resolve group problems and encouraging the group to work together?

It is possible that you may take on any of these roles during a session. Try to be proactive (initiating learning) as well as reactive (responding to problems). Your role in the group should be to challenge and support. By circulating around the groups you will be able to differentiate the group tasks. You can challenge some groups by questioning, by introducing new themes or materials, and give extra differentiated support to others. It is much more difficult to challenge than to support so you may need, at the planning stage, to consider how you would extend the activity for some learners.

Assessing group work
How will you assess your learners individually and collaboratively against the learning outcomes? The chapter on assessment will help you in this but there are particular considerations to be addressed in the assessment of a group work activity.

• **Group presentation.** If the group is required to give a presentation on their learning to the other groups, either you and/or the other learners (peers) could assess them, using pre-published criteria. This may work well if the learners are mature enough to assess each other. Peer assessment is addressed in a later chapter, but in using this method of assessment for group work, learners must be reassured that the weighting of the peer-assessed grade in relation to the programme as a whole is appropriate.

• **Individual assignments.** Each learner completes an individual piece of work, perhaps evaluating the group-work exercise. This ensures that the individual's contribution to the whole process can be assessed. However, it should be noted that it does not always give an accurate assessment of the process: some people are much better at doing something than writing about it.

In choosing your method of assessment you should consider your original learning purposes and ensure that the assignment assesses the intended learning. This sounds obvious but is sometimes more difficult to achieve. For example, is your prime objective for learners to work together or to produce a product? Are you more interested in the process the learners go through or the product of the activity?

5.2 Raising self-esteem and motivating learners

Raising self-esteem
Self-esteem is the way in which we perceive our worth in terms of what we hold to be important. Thus, if sports skills are given high status in a particular social and or family circle, and one child cannot learn those skills, s/he will perceive him/herself to be less successful than others. Furthermore, on perceiving him/herself to be poor at sport s/he may build up a negative attitude towards sport activities and attack any new situation with a lack of confidence, thus making failure more likely. Similarly with other kinds of learning: if learners perceive themselves to be

unsuccessful, they will have low self-esteem and will lack confidence in their own ability to learn something new. A person with high self-esteem will be more willing to 'have a go' and not be afraid to make mistakes. This has many implications for you as a teacher. The more you can raise your learners' self-esteem, the more confident they will be and the more positive an atmosphere is built up in the classroom.

How do you do this? There are two basic ways:

- by ensuring learners succeed
- by building a positive ethos in the classroom where learners are not afraid of making mistakes and want to learn.

(See **Task Two**.)

TASK TWO

Analyse the ways in which you build your learners' self-esteem.

1. Do you plan for your **learners to succeed** by:

- Ensuring the material presented is at the correct level for them?
- Making assessment criteria clear and preparing learners for assignments?
- Giving positive constructive feedback, verbal and written, to indicate what learners have to do to improve their grading?
- Relating assessment clearly to course work
- Considering all types of learners in your planning?

---

2. Do you build a **positive classroom ethos** by:

• Spending time at the start of the programme to allow learners to get to know each other, positively emphasising the importance of knowing and using names?
• Encouraging learners to question, discuss, participate and support each other?
• Giving learners the opportunity to respond in a variety of ways, e.g. within a small group so they can try out new ideas before presenting them to the whole group?
   • Giving learners the opportunity to discuss the content of the programme so they can feel ownership?
• Encouraging learners to work with different people in different groups?
• Valuing your learners – listening and responding to them as individuals?

Motivating learners

In order to motivate your learners you should consider why they are on the programme and how they learn. The former of these is addressed under the heading 'mismatch of expectation' (see below) and the latter in Chapter 2. There are other factors involved. There are various taxonomies of levels of motivation which are helpful in generic terms. Maslow (1987) identifies different levels of need ranging from the basic physical needs of humans to higher order needs. He theorises that unless basic needs are met, for instance the need to feel physically comfortable, humans are not motivated to learn. Thus it is important for teachers to ensure that learners have enough 'comfort breaks' to move around, go to the toilet and refresh themselves with food and drink. Motivation is also analysed in terms of intrinsic or extrinsic motivation (see Chapter 2). Thus young children will initially be extrinsically motivated by the need to please important people, e.g. their parents or teachers. Praise is therefore particularly important here. However, in adulthood, when there are many other pressures on learners, it is hoped that learning itself will become intrinsically motivating, i.e. learners will want to learn because the material itself is motivating, interesting and potentially of value. Think about what motivates you? When you are learning, perhaps by listening to a lecture or watching a television programme about a new topic, what is it that maintains your interest level? Is it:

- Good quality visual material that helps you to understand?
- An enthusiastic presenter?
- The use of humour?
- Examples from the presenter's own experience to which you can relate?
- Material directly related to your own context?
- An unusual presentation that changes its focus and methods?

Many of the above will motivate your learners and as you get to know them and the content of the programme you are teaching, you will find ways of presenting your material in a stimulating and motivating way.

5.3 Managing behaviour

One of the major concerns for many new teachers is that of behaviour management. 'Will I be able to control the learners?'

The first principle to consider is the aim of discipline. Why do we want our learners to be disciplined? You may agree with some of the following answers:

- It is a social skill which all adults must learn.
- To enable learners eventually to learn self-discipline.
- To allow other learners to learn.
- To allow the teacher to teach.

All these reasons are valid. The main reason we need discipline in the classroom is for learners to learn. In order for a group to learn there must be an acknowledgement of a common framework of behaviour. At first sight this may seem obvious; of course we want learners to learn. However, if this aim is our first principle, there is an implicit understanding that our aim is not necessarily for learners to sit still, listen and generally follow to the letter every instruction we give. We must allow learners some autonomy and set limits which are sensitive to their needs in order for that learning to take place.

Classroom rules

The most effective classroom rules are those which are made collaboratively by teachers and learners at the beginning of the course. They can easily be established either formally or informally according to the group size, maturity or other context. They usually address the following issues:

- punctuality
- respecting others' contributions in class
- bringing the correct materials
- listening to others
- only one person speaking at a time.

The rules should be framed in the positive rather than the negative, to make it clear to learners what they should do rather than what they should not do. Once established, any breach can be referred to the rules, rather than personalising the problem between the learner and the teacher.

TASK THREE

Choose four rules you would like to introduce and implement in one of the groups which you teach.

1.

2.

3.

4.

Positive teaching

We all respond better when people are positive to us rather than negative. A behavioural approach to teaching acknowledges that positive reinforcement of a behaviour increases the likelihood of its reoccurrence. Thus praise is an important part of any teacher's repertoire and builds a positive classroom ethos. Of course, praise must be used carefully with adult learners to ensure it does not become patronising. It may be more effective to praise in private, at the end of the session, rather than in front of peers. The praise should indicate what the learner has done well and should sometimes be related to effort as well as achievement. Praise should always be sincere and genuine and never gushing, but should be used for all learners at some time.

A positive classroom ethos is one which inspires trust in learners so that they are not afraid to tackle new subjects or attempt answers to questions when they may be wrong. The need to feel safe is a basic human instinct and one which must be satisfied before learning can take place. Positive teaching emphasises success rather than failure.

Mismatch of expectation
Learners come to learning programmes for a variety of reasons. Which of these apply to your learners:

* to gain a qualification
* to do their existing job better
* sent by employer
* unable to remain at school
* to update skills
* for retraining?

Whatever the reasons, there may be a mismatch of expectation between what you are about to deliver and what they expect from such a programme. You may assume all learners are highly motivated to succeed and be intensely interested in your subject. Whereas for the learner this course may not have been their choice. Such a mismatch can lead to low motivation and disaffection. At the beginning of a programme it is useful to clearly spell out the rationale, the content and the teaching methods involved. At such a time it is also useful to identify learners' expectations and hopes for the programme so that you all move forward to a common agenda.

First encounters
The first time you meet a group of learners is very important. First impressions always lay the foundation for future relationships and can be difficult to alter, once established. Before you meet a group of learners you should ask yourself.

1. What kind of relationship do I want with them?
    How formal should I be? It is better to begin more formally and relax over time than vice versa. At this stage you know little about their expectations of you and you need to find out more about them before you can accurately judge how they will respond to you.

2. What do I know about them already?
    What information can I find out about them from other teachers? What does your own experience tell you about similar groups?

3. How can I best project a positive ethos and convey positive expectations for the group and for the programme?

4. How can I find out about their existing knowledge? (See Chapter 2.)

5.   How can I ensure that the material I cover initially is at the correct level?

6.   How can I get to know mt learners?
     For some groups that you teach you will not have time to get to know them, either because the groups are too large or because the programmes you deliver are too short. However, it is very important, wherever possible, to learn their names. Initially, you can ask learners to put a card with their name on the table in front of them or use sticky labels which they can wear. Being able to use names when you question or respond to learners immediately gives you power and is the beginning of a relationship. In the longer term you should endeavour to learn names.

A model of behaviour management

Bill Rogers (1997) offers a useful model for teachers to follow in planning for behaviour management. It is written primarily for schools but the principles are appropriate for any age group. Well-managed sessions are carefully planned. They do not just happen (see Chapter 4). There is no doubt that what the teacher does influences the behaviour of the learners, but effective management techniques can be learned by all teachers. Research has shown that it is not the major behaviour problems that hinder good teaching and learning in the classroom but the small problems that frequently occur such as learners butting in, or hindering others. These are the common misdemeanours that happen frequently and that teachers find most troublesome.

The following model is based upon Rogers (1997) and addresses behaviour management in three phases, preventative, responsive and those which seek to build positive classroom relationships.

1. Preventative strategies

Good classroom management skills minimise the likelihood of disruption in the classroom. They ensure that routines are in place which make clear to learners what is expected of them and they ensure that the session is well-planned so that the teacher has clear intentions and can maintain a good pace.

The following questions form a checklist which you can use to ensure that your planning takes into account the management of the session.

- Is the beginning of the session well paced to engage learners' attention from the start?
- Are resources ready, working and accessible?
- Is the room layout appropriate to the session and the learners?
- Is there a balance in teaching methods to maintain learners' concentration?
- Is the subject matter relevant to learners?
- Are explanations carefully thought through to ensure learners understand what

they have to do?
- Is the session pitched at the correct level for the learners?
- Are there extension activities for learners who finish quickly?
- Is there time built into the session when you can give support to individuals or groups?

2. Responsive strategies

During the session the role of the teacher is to manage the group to ensure that learning takes place. In spite of the most careful planning, there may be minor disruptions caused by individuals or groups when you will need to intervene and bring learners back on task.

It is important to do this in a way which does not demean, nor put you in a potentially conflicting situation where either your self-esteem or that of the learner is damaged.

There are a number of strategies you can use at different stages of disruption as appropriate:

- ignoring minimal inappropriate behaviour; in the hope that it may simply die away
- reminding of or referring to simple rules
- referring back to the task
- reprimands
- giving choices, e.g. 'would you rather do this task now or do some individual work now and complete the task later?'

3. Building relationships

The importance of the first meeting with learners has already been discussed. This should form only the beginning of the relationship you build with your learners. Teaching and learning is a very personal process and is bound up with the interpersonal relationships you have with your learners. A teacher needs to decide what kind of relationship s/he will have and how that relationship can be formed and maintained. This may be difficult when timetabling constraints may mean that learners and teacher depart quickly after a session or meet only infrequently.

There are, however, many opportunities for the individual interaction which forms relationships, either in-class or out. Time can be made for brief exchanges at the end of sessions. It is particularly important to follow up any particular incidents which may have happened, either positive or negative. A teacher needs to remain in tune with learners and aware of any external influences there may be on their learning (see Chapter 2). S/he may use tutorial time to get to know learners or allow some time to talk about common interests. Learners should see teachers as people to whom they can relate.

5.4 The role of language in learning

Jargon

Any communication is only effective if both parties share a common language. You will already have discovered that there is much jargon in use in education itself as well as the technical terminology relating to your own subject. Such terminology is obvious to the expert but may prevent the learner from accessing what you have to say. There are three ways in which you can address this problem:

- at the start of a programme, distribute a glossary to your learners
- before a session, consider what terms you will use and ensure that your learners will have been introduced to them
- most importantly, encourage your learners to ask when they do not understand a term.

You should also encourage them to explain terms as they use them.

Explaining

Clear explanations are a key feature of effective teaching (see **Task Four**).

TASK FOUR

Think of an explanation that you have used recently and analyse it against the following features:

- Was the level of language appropriate to the group? ....
- Were all technical terms explained? ....
- Was it short and concise enough to maintain interest? ....
- Did I start from what the learners already knew? ....
- Did I use questions to check understanding? ....
- Did I give several examples in different contexts to help learners to generalise? ....
- Did I relate it to other experiences of the group? ....
- Did I pace it correctly to maintain momentum while giving time for queries? ....

5.5 Meeting individual needs: the inclusive classroom

We have already acknowledged in Chapter 2 that within any group of learners there is a wide range of needs as each learner is individual and different. There are also learners who are sometimes referred to as having special needs. This may at first appear a precise definition but on closer examination it is not as helpful as it seems. There are many learners in employment and in further and higher education who need special support and this may take a variety of different forms, e.g. a separate curriculum, different resources, different aids to learning etc. However, different learners need different support at different times in their education and training and it is thus more difficult than it first appears to distinguish whose needs are special and what is special as opposed to what is ordinary.

There are many texts which focus on these issues and any teacher should make sure that s/he is familiar with the learning support available in their organisation. Most large organisations have resources and expertise that can help the teacher to support the learners.

The concept of **Inclusive Education** which is currently widely used, and which has been defined by the Tomlinson Report (FEFC, 1996) and many equal opportunity policies, is one which is very relevant in all areas of post-16 education and training. Inclusive Education assumes that all learners need support to learn. We know that all learners are different and thus teachers must provide different kinds of support for them at the different stages of the programme. Some learners may need extra resources, some may need extra help with particular concepts, some may need extra help with language. With the support of their own organisation the teacher should use the appropriate methods and resources to ensure that all learners learn.

Summary

Having planned for the most appropriate teaching and learning strategies which lead to your learning outcomes, your role in the session is to manage those strategies and the learners themselves. This requires considerable skill in analysing the responses of learners and being able to vary your approach without losing sight of your original intentions. This chapter addressed various ways in which you can achieve this.

Whether you teach large or small groups, there are a number of issues to address in your role as the teacher.

* What will you do during the sessions?
* How can you ensure that your actions build the positive classroom atmosphere necessary for all your learners to succeed?

As a teacher you also have to examine your own philosophy and style of teaching. This chapter encourages you to reflect on your own attitudes to the management of behaviour and provides you with a model on which to base the strategies you use.

Teaching the Post-16 Learner

By reading previous chapters you should now be aware that all learners are different. The concept of Inclusive Education and Training embodies this truism and seeks to support all learners. It shifts the emphasis from what is 'the norm' and what is 'special' to meeting the needs of all learners within the programmes we provide.

References and further reading

General
FENTO (1999) *Standards for Teaching and Supporting Learning in Further Education in England and Wales*. London: FENTO.

Managing learning
Brown, H. and Benson, S. (eds) (1992) *A Practical Guide to Working with People with Learning Disabilities: a Handbook for Care Assistants and Support Workers*. London: Hawker Publications.
Further Education Funding Council (1996) *Inclusive Learning: A Report of the Committee on Students with Learning Difficulties and/or Disabilities*. Coventry: FEFC.
Gibbs, G. (1995) *Learning in Teams: a Tutor Guide*. Oxford: Oxford Centre for Staff Development.
Jaques, D. (1984) *Learning in Groups*. London: Croom Helm.
Maslow, A.H. (1987) 3rd edn. *Motivation and Personality*. London: Harper and Row.
Rogers, A. (1996) *Teaching Adults*. Milton Keynes: Open University Press.
Rogers, B. (1997) 2nd edn. *You Know the Fair Rule*. London: Pitman.
Wolfendale, S. and Corbett, J. (eds) (1996) *Opening Doors: Learning Support in Higher Education*. London: Cassell.

6

Assessing Your Learners

- competence-based assessment
- assessment of prior (experiential) learning (AP(E)L)
- self- and peer assessment
- giving feedback and recording learner achievement.

The FENTO Standards addressed in this chapter

Many aspects of Key Area F – Assessing the outcomes of learning and learners' achievements – (as related to assessing learners' achievements) are addressed in this chapter. For example:

F1 Use appropriate assessment methods to measure learning and achievement

(a) identify an appropriate range of assessment methods which will deliver fair, valid and reliable results

(e) create realistic and relevant assessment activities that encourage learning as well as assessing specified outcomes that meet college and external requirements

(g) use an appropriate variety of valid and reliable assessment procedures that are credible and compatible with the learning programme and the required learning outcomes

(k) ensure that learners are provided with clear and constructive feedback on assessment outcomes within an appropriate timescale

Critical understanding and essential knowledge:

- distinctions between formative and summative assessment procedures
- the purpose of self, peer and tutor assessments and how these methods of assessment relate to each other
- competence-based and non-competence-based methods of assessment
- the appropriate timing and pace of assessment within a learning programme

F2 Make use of assessment information

(a) use continuous assessment to help individual learners assess their progress and identify learning issues

(b) use assessment information to assess how far learning objectives have been achieved

Critical understanding and essential knowledge

• continuous assessment and end-of-programme assessment processes, and when to use them

In addition an aspect of Key Area A (A?h) is addressed in this chapter as we have discussed how to 'provide feedback to the learner on the outcome of the assessment and its consequences'.

We have also provided an overview of AP(E)L which is included in various parts of the standards.

6.1 Different types and techniques of assessment

The two types of assessment are **formative** and **summative**. Often the same **techniques** can be use for both, but it is the **purpose** of assessment which is different.

Summative assessment is used at the end of a course, module or topic and contributes towards the learner's final certificate or award. Summative assessment can have different purposes and is used by different people for different purposes. For example:

• learners may use it to help them select further courses

• colleges may use it to help select learners for their courses

• organisations may use it as part of a curriculum review and as a way of evaluating the course and its teachers

• employers use it in selecting employees

• examining bodies use it as the basis of awarding their qualifications.

More recently summative assessment has been used by the government to compare organisations, locally and nationally, which has led to the annual publication of 'league tables'.

Formative assessment is that which helps in the teaching and learning process by being diagnostic. The advantages of employing formative assessment techniques are given in the chapter outline.

The **techniques** you use to assess learners will vary according to the subject you teach and the preferences of the body which awards the qualification. The following are the most commonly used assessment techniques:

- assignments
- end examination
- essays
- fieldwork
- multiple choice
- observation
- practical work
- projects (individual or group)
- question and answer
- quiz
- reports
- seminars.

The techniques listed can be used in various combinations. For example, you may ask learners to write a report on a fieldwork experience or you may observe their practical work.

With the exception of the end examination, which is only used for summative purposes, all other techniques can be used for either formative or summative purposes, but the focus or process may be different. You may find that in your own subject area other assessment techniques are employed and, as already stated, you will probably have little or no control over the way summative assessment is carried out.

However, with formative assessment you do have a choice. At times your formative assessment should mirror the summative assessment. So, if learners have to take an unseen end examination you should ensure they have a mock exam to prepare them for the real thing, whether this be a multiple choice paper or an essay-based exam. However, it is important that there is variety in the assessment techniques employed – a class which is continually given mock exams will get very fed up with them!

As well as mirroring the summative in the formative assessment, you need to match it to the characteristics of the group and the individuals within it. If a class is competitive, a quiz may motivate them, but beware of encouraging too much competition in a group as this can have unforeseen consequences. Assessment should be challenging but not so difficult that learners fail and become demotivated. Getting the right balance is not always easy, especially if the class has a large range in ability levels, but as you get to know these abilities, and those of individuals within it, you can tailor the techniques and level of assessment so as to challenge, but not demotivate, all. Remember that individuals learn in different ways (see Chapter 2) and therefore they benefit from different types of assessment.

6.2 Validity and reliability

When discussing assessment, **validity** and **reliability** are often mentioned together as if they are the same thing. They are not.

- **Validity** is about the appropriateness of the assessment – whether it tests what it is supposed to test.
- **Reliability** is concerned with whether a test consistently measures what it is supposed to measure.

Validity can be divided into two types: validity of **content** coverage, i.e. are you assessing across the curriculum or just a small part of it; validity of **technique,** i.e. does the way you assess actually test what it purports to be (see example about wiring a 13-amp plug, below)?

To have **content** validity you need to ensure that any assessment you devise covers all (or a representative sample) of the curriculum to which it relates. If working as a member of a team is considered to be an important aspect of a group-work project, then this aspect of the affective domain needs to be measured in some way by the assessment.

There is no easy guide to choosing the right technique to ensure this type of validity. As a professional teacher it is part of your role to devise assessments which do measure what you want them to. You should bear in mind that different techniques are appropriate to measure achievement within the three domains (discussed in Chapter 2) – It would be inappropriate to use a multiple-choice paper to assess how well a nursery nurse learner was able to interact with children.

TASK ONE

Consider which techniques would be valid in the three domains (some may appear in more than one) within your own subject area.

- assignments
- end examination
- essays
- fieldwork
- multiple-choice test
- observation

- practical work
- projects (individual or group)
- question and answer
- quiz
- reports
- seminars

Cognitive	Affective	Psycho-motor

Reliability is about whether the assessment would produce the same results if:

- it was marked by different assessors
- the same person assessed it at different times
- the same learner takes the test at different times.

More objective assessment techniques, such as multiple-choice questions, generally have a higher reliability than more subjective techniques, such as writing an essay. But it is not appropriate to use objective testing at all times. For any kind of assessment you need to have some kind of marking scheme as this increases reliability. Therefore, the person designing the assessment should also design a marking scheme so that it is clear what s/he intended the learners to produce and to give guidance to different assessors assessing the same work.

If we mark some learners' work one day and others the next we may have changed our ideas on what we wanted from the assessment. A properly designed marking scheme makes this less likely and therefore more reliable. It may be appropriate to assign the proportion of marks to be allocated to each aspect of the assessment.

TASK TWO

Using an assessment you have recently given to a group of learners, devise a marking scheme for this as if you were having to share the marking with a colleague.

Some courses have cover sheets for their coursework assessments. These can increase reliability if they contain guidance for learners or assessors on how the work should be assessed. If you have responsibility for a course which does not use any kind of cover sheet you might consider designing one to suit your purposes. Don't necessarily expect it to work immediately as you may need to modify it in the light of experience.

6.3 Assessing to meet objectives

The techniques used in assessing must be appropriate to what it is you are intending to assess. For example, in an electrical installation course, if you wish to know whether a learner knows the correct colour for earth, neutral and live wires, you could give a written test. If, however, you want to know if s/he can correctly wire a 13-amp plug, you should set a practical task to assess the practical skills involved in actually wiring the plug.

Teachers often make the mistake of not matching the assessment to the objectives and therefore the assessment is not valid, i.e. it does not assess what it purports to do. So if you assessed a learner's practical ability to wire a 13-amp plug by giving a multiple-choice test asking what colour wires are which, your assessment would not be valid.

TASK THREE

Using the list of techniques here, and with reference to one course which you teach, fill in the columns stating:

• whether you use the technique (column a)
• for what objective(s) (column b)
• whether your use of them is valid for meeting those objective(s) (column c)
• what improvement you could make in assessing that objective (column d).

Technique	(a) Use?	(b) Objective(s)?	(b) Valid?	(d) Improvement?
Assignments				
Formal examination				
Essays				
Fieldwork				
Multiple choice				
Observation				
Practical tests				
Projects (individual)				
Projects (group)				
Questions and answers				
Quiz				
Report				
Seminars				
Other (state technique)				

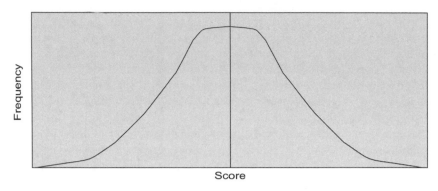

Figure 6.1 Normal distribution curve

6.4 Referencing type

There are two types of referencing in assessment: **norm referencing** and **criterion referencing**.

Norm referencing is where marks are allocated to achieve a normal curve of distribution. This means that a small percentage gain a high grade and a small percentage fail, while the majority are awarded an average mark (see Figure 6.1). Externally set, unseen end examinations often employ this type of marking regime whereby marks are adjusted to ensure a normal distribution. This has led to the belief that it is easier to pass certain examinations in some years than in others.

In classes employing norm referencing it is likely that all the learners will be assessed on the same thing at the same time. If all are of similar ability and work at the same pace, this arrangement will work. However, if you have a class with mixed ability, the more able or faster learners will consistently do better while the less able or slower learners will perform less well, perhaps because they have not had enough time to master the material on which they are being assessed.

If the course you teach has coursework assessments, it may be part of your job, as a professional teacher, to decide when to assess the class, or individuals within it, on a particular aspect. Formative assessment of the class, and of individuals, will help you do this, although the timing may be dictated by a course timetable or by the awarding body's requirements.

Criterion-referenced assessment is where learners are required to demonstrate an understanding or knowledge in a number of set criteria or objectives. Their achievement is judged only against these criteria and not in relation to other learners, so all can get 100 per cent or all can get 0 per cent.

If you work on a course which employs a criterion-referenced framework, you may have a group being assessed on different aspects and at different stages of the subject. Once they have demonstrated their knowledge or skills in a particular area they can then progress to the next stage, irrespective of progress of others in the class. This arrangement makes it necessary for a teacher to be able to switch from one aspect to another quickly and effectively so that no individual is disadvantaged. Again a well-planned formative assessment schedule can help you to know when an individual is ready to be assessed on a particular aspect.

6.5 Competence-based assessment

This is a development from criterion-referenced assessment whereby the 'syllabus' for a 'course' consists of a set of performance criteria in which learners have to demonstrate their competence. This type of assessment has been used for decades but it is only since the late 1980s that it has gained much ground in this country. In 1986 the government set up the National Council for Vocational Qualifications (NCVQ) to look at rationalising the whole area of vocational qualifications, of which there were literally hundreds. What developed was a system of vocationally based standards devised by bodies made up of employers and others involved in training and assessment. These are called National Vocational Qualifications (NVQs) and are available at five levels (from entry level worker to senior management) and in many vocational areas. NVQs were designed to be gained by those in employment by work-based assessment allowing learners (sometimes called candidates) to demonstrate the skills they have in relation to their job.

Since their introduction NVQs have become very accepted in some vocational areas (replacing all the more traditional qualifications) but have hardly touched others. They have also been praised by many, for their contribution in enabling those in work to gain qualifications for the skills they already have, but criticised by other commentators for a number of reasons. This is not the place to discuss the relative merits and disadvantages of NVQs, although commentators on both sides of the argument are included in the list of further reading at the end of the chapter.

If you work in the post-16 sector of education and training, you will not have missed the debate about NVQs. The use of NVQs within further education and other training organisations has meant a change in the role of the teacher. One major change which NVQs have brought about is that assessment is now at the forefront of some learning situations.

Candidates working towards achieving NVQs have to compile a portfolio of evidence to demonstrate their competence in the performance criteria related to the elements and units they are taking. In addition, because of the importance of work-based assessment many teachers now have to assess within the workplace or in a simulated workplace (sometimes called Real Work Environment (RWE)) such as hairdressing salons or training restaurants.

Those teachers working with NVQs are required to become qualified assessors themselves, demonstrating their own competence in the assessment process by taking two units from the Training and Development standards (D32 and D33). As an example of how NVQs are designed, one element from the D32 unit (Assess Candidate Performance) is reproduced in Figure 6.2.

D321 *Identify Opportunities for the Collection of Evidence of Competent Performance*
  (a) the opportunities identified are relevant to the element(s) to be assessed
  (b) best use is made of naturally occurring evidence and related questioning before alternatives are considered
  (c) advice is sought when alternative evidence is proposed
  (d) opportunities are selected to minimise disruption to normal activity
  (e) opportunities are selected to ensure access to fair and reliable assessment
  (f) a resulting assessment plan is discussed and agreed with candidate and others who may be affected

Figure 6.2 Example of performance criteria from the
National Standards for Training and Development

Once a tutor has gained D32 and D33 s/he is qualified to assess NVQs in their subject area. Where NVQs are being used, the organisation should have a policy and procedure to enable staff working with NVQs to become qualified assessors. To ensure greater reliability, NVQ awarding bodies employ a process of internal and external verification and there are further units in the training and development standards for those undertaking internal and external verification (D34 and D35).

6.6 Assessment of Prior (Experiential) Learning (AP(E)L)

Another result of the introduction of competence-based learning (but not restricted to it) is the area of **assessment of prior learning** (APL) and **assessment of prior experiential learning** (APEL). This is a way whereby people can get credit for **previous courses** they have taken (APL) or **prior experience** which has meant they have gained the skills/knowledge required by the awarding body (AP(E)L).

APL is used where there is a certificate of learning which can be verified as equivalent to the credit being claimed. APEL is used where the learning has not involved formal courses but can nevertheless be verified. In relation to NVQs, APEL is very important as it is what a person can do, and knows, rather than the courses s/he has attended which is important. Some organisations have assessment centres whereby people can be assessed against the relevant standards by qualified assessors. In other cases individuals may need help in developing a portfolio to show evidence of their achievement before they can be assessed. Staff working in this area need a further unit from the training and development standards (D36).

However, it is not only those working with NVQs or with official AP(E)L who need to be aware of and familiar with this concept. In almost every class you will have learners with varied experiences both in terms of previous educational achievements and life experiences.

This is especially true with adults but should not be ignored even with the younger, less mature learners. In the past these experiences were ignored and everyone in the class had to do the same work even if it was too easy for them or a repetition of what they had already done, which meant they could became demotivated. Now it is necessary to take these experiences into account when planning your sessions (see previous chapters) and by assessing learners' knowledge and skills you can develop differentiated tasks to enable everyone in the class to learn from them and thus remain motivated.

When you develop a profile of your learners (Chapter 2) you need to include a way of ascertaining the background of your learners in terms of their previous qualifications and experiences. If you use a questionnaire you will probably have asked for qualifications and (if appropriate) work experiences, current and past. You could also include a question asking them to identify their previous experiences which may be relevant to the current course.

Another method of doing this is to have the learners introduce themselves to the rest of the class, to include the previous experiences relevant to the course. If this might embarrass individuals you can ask each one to interview another learner and then introduce that person to the rest of the class. This will help you pick up on any relevant experiences which you can follow up with the individual if necessary.

TASK FOUR

For the class you profiled in Chapter 2, devise a way of ascertaining their prior learning and experiences which may be relevant to the course.

6.7 Self- and peer assessment

Traditionally it is teachers who assess learners. Even with external examinations the assessors are usually teachers. The development of self- and peer assessment is a departure from this traditional process and is viewed with suspicion by some in the educational world. However, it can provide exciting and challenging experiences which encourage and motivate learners.

Self- and peer assessment have been used in all sectors of education, including primary schools. In further and higher education some subject areas have been more innovative in introducing some form of self- and peer assessment and in some cases the marks given by self and peer contribute towards the final grade for the piece of work. Where self, peer and teacher engage in a collaborative assessment exercise, this is called **triadic** assessment.

Most learners engage in some form of **self-assessment** when they read through a completed assignment or project and revise it before submission.

They can further be encouraged to engage in self-assessment by having to include a written self-assessment with their submitted work. It might be that their self-assessment is used only as an indication to the teacher that they have done this, and as an encouragement for them to revise work before submission, but in some courses self-assessment can contribute towards the mark given for a piece of work (see above).

In this case, wouldn't all learners give themselves 100 per cent? Research into this shows that learners usually give themselves very similar marks to those of the teacher, with poorer learners underestimating their marks. Obviously the amount of self-assessment which can contribute to final marks will depend on the structure of the course you teach, but even if you cannot introduce it as part of the summative assessment you can use it to help your learners be more self-assessing about their work before submitting it and thereby give them the best chance of achieving at their highest capability.

There are many examples of **peer assessment** – again in all sectors of education, including primary schools. Often it is a process whereby older children work with and assess younger children, but it can be used in classes whereby learners assess their classmates.

In most courses there is now an element of learners working together, whether this be in informal discussion groups or more formally in pair or group-work practicals, projects or assignments. If the process they are engaged in is part of what is being assessed, it is unlikely that the teacher will be able to observe all that goes on during group-work activities. In this case peer assessment is a way of assessing what the teacher cannot assess.

Learners can also assess the work of others in their class – they have engaged in the work themselves so it could be argued they are best placed to assess the same work by other learners. Critics of peer assessment claim that learners will overgrade their peers leading to inflated marks. However, research into this shows that peers give broadly similar marks to teachers and if the process is well planned the advantages to both assessed and assessor are many. Peer assessment is often accompanied by peer tutoring and if you are not able to introduce peer assessment into your course, because of regulations, you may be able to use peer tutoring.

Here are some examples of advantages given by those who have taken part in peer tutoring/assessment:

- improves attainment for both assessor and assessee
- tutor/assessor reviews and consolidates knowledge as well as developing greater insight into subject
- one-to-one attention for tutee/assessee
- developing sense of personal esteem for tutor/assessor
- verbal and social improvement for both parties
- companionship. (Adapted from Topping, 1988).

There are a number of books on peer tutoring and assessment given in the list of further reading at the end of this chapter.

If you want to introduce an element of self- and peer assessment into the course you teach there are a number of things to consider. It needs to be thoroughly planned and the process needs to be explained carefully to the learners, together with the advantages, to them, of engaging in the process. If they think you are doing it to lessen your workload they are unlikely to look on it positively. It is very helpful to have specific assessment criteria for the piece of work being peer-assessed. Many courses do have these but if they do not exist for the course on which you teach, you can involve the learners in devising criteria to be used. In this case it may be helpful to give them an example to work from. An example of an assessment grid can be found in *Strategies for Diversifying Assessment in Higher Education* by Brown, Rust and Gibbs (1994).

TASK FIVE

For the class you have profiled (Chapter 2):

• Devise a way to encourage them to engage in self-assessment for one piece of work.

• Devise a process of peer tutoring and assessment (if this cannot be built into the formal assessment then it can be done as part of the formative assessment).

If you are trying this for the first time with a class it is useful to evaluate the process after completion. This might include asking learners how they felt about the process and comparing the marks given by self and/or peer with your own. If the process does not work the first time, do not be discouraged. It can often take learners, and teachers, some time before they are comfortable with a departure from the traditional approach to assessment. If you persevere you will become more confident and comfortable with the process and the benefits to the learners will become evident and they, in turn, will accept it.

6.8 Giving feedback and recording learner achievement

Giving feedback
Teachers give feedback to learners all the time. In class the tone of your voice or your stance can indicate much to learners in regard to how you feel about them and the answers they give or the work they have done. We should not underestimate the importance of these non-verbal communications. Giving effective feedback, both for informal assessment such as questions asked in the class and on formal coursework, is a skill that all teachers need to develop. Feedback should not demotivate learners and should also give an indication of what they can do to improve.

In the classroom assessment may take place in the form of questions to the class which should be relevant to the topic and at a level where the learners can be expected to know the answer.

Questions to the whole class can be used to ascertain general understanding, but often this means that the same few individuals answer all the time. While you need to be aware of some individuals' shyness, in speaking in front of others, you can direct questions at specific learners by using their names and asking other, more vocal, individuals to give others a chance to answer. This need not be confrontational if handled properly.

When addressing an individual try to be sure that s/he will be able to answer, at least in part, the question as this provides motivation, especially for less able learners. Ensure also you give thinking time. This may mean that there is silence in the class for some seconds (seconds can feel like hours to teachers who are used to having some sound at all times) but learners may need time to formulate answers before speaking.

It may be necessary to give hints or clues if a learner is struggling with an answer and you may want to ask a supplementary question to stretch the thinking of the class or individual respondent.

Often pair or group-work activities, such as discussions, are reported back to the whole class. This needs sensitive handling in terms of feedback. In this situation you need to ensure that all pairs/groups listen to their classmates and respect their contributions. You may want to ask questions to probe their understanding of what they have been working on. If one person is to report back for the group try to ensure that it is not the same person every time. The shyer members of the group can be encouraged to give feedback on the group's behalf – often it is easier for him/ her to do this as it is not their own individual views or ideas they are expressing, but those of the group.

Feedback on written work may be given verbally, but more usually it is given in writing. In the past lists of the marks were printed and displayed for all to see. This was good for those who got good marks but demotivated those who did not do so well. While learners may share their marks or feedback with each other this should be their choice and not yours. When returning work give it out alphabetically rather than from the top mark to the bottom – it can be demotivating always to be the last to get your work back.

Written feedback should be clear and if you are allocating a grade or mark you should always say how that mark was arrived at.

Reference to any specific assessment criteria can help if these are part of the course on which you teach. A good guide is the 'sandwich' approach whereby you:

- say something good about the piece of work
- make comments on how it could be improved
- comment on its merits.

Feedback should be given as quickly as possible after submission – some departments or sections have a time specified for return of assessed work. This means that you need to organise your time so that you can mark the work in the required time. Some FE colleges are now experimenting with assessment weeks whereby teaching is suspended for that period of time to enable staff to mark the work at the end of module, unit, term or semester.

Whatever you are giving feedback on, it needs to be done in such a way as to motivate the learners. You should:

- praise what they have done well
- say what is incorrect
- give guidance on what they could do to improve the piece of work.

Recording learner achievement
This is an important aspect of the teacher's role especially on courses which employ coursework as the main, or only, method of assessment. It is these marks which make up the learner's final grade. There are numerous ways of recording achievement – almost as many as there are departments and training organisations. Make sure you are aware of the recording process within the departments or faculties in which you work and adhere to them. Try to enter marks or grades as soon as possible and do not leave it all to the last minute. Panic at the end of the

course can be avoided if you are well organised in this area.

As well as the official recording of learner achievement required by the department or organisation, you should keep your own records of learner achievement. In this way you will know which learners have achieved what in terms of objectives covered or pieces of work completed.

Again there are many different ways of doing this, and you will need to develop your own procedure which works for you and the types of assessment your learners undertake. However you do this, it must be systematic and easy to understand. Ideally it should give you, at a glance, an overview of what each learner has achieved at any time within the course.

Summary

In this chapter we have looked at many aspects of assessment and you have (hopefully) completed the tasks which have been included. You should now be aware of the following aspects of assessment:

- different types and techniques of assessment
- validity and reliability
- assessing to meet objectives
- referencing type – norm and criterion referencing
- competence-based assessment
- assessment of prior (experiential) learning (AP(E)L)
- self- and peer assessment
- giving feedback and recording learner achievement.

It is, as always, important that you are able to relate what you have learnt about assessment to your own learners and teaching situation. Assessment is an important aspect of work of all teachers and by understanding its complex nature you will be better able to assess your learners fairly, reliably and competently and thus enhance their learning in your subject area.

References and further reading

General
FENTO (1999) *Standards for Teaching and Supporting Learning in Further Education in England and Wales.* London: FENTO.

Competence-based learning
Beaumont, G. (1995) *Review of 100 NVQs and SVQs.* London: DfEE.
Burchell, H. and Woolhouse, M. (1995) Learner autonomy in competence based post-compulsory teacher education, *British Journal of In-service Training*, Vol. 21, no. 2.

Capey, J. (1995) *GNVQ Assessment Review: Final Report of the Review Group.* London: NCVQ.
Chown, A. (1992) TDLB standards in FE, *Journal of Further and Higher Education*, Vol. 16, no. 13, Autumn.
Employment Department (1991) *National Standards for Training and Development.*
Hodkinson, P. (1992) Alternative models of competence in vocational education and training, *Journal of Further and Higher Education*, Vol. 16, no. 2, Summer.
Hyland, T. (1994) *Competence, Education and NVQs: Dissenting Perspectives.* London: Cassell.
Norris, N. (1991) The trouble with competence. *Cambridge Journal of Education*, Vol. 21, no. 3.
Wolf, A. (1993) *Assessment Issues and Problems in Criterion-based Systems.* London: FEU.

Self- and peer assessment

Brown, S. and Dove, P. (1991) *Self and Peer Assessment.* SCED Paper 63.
Brown, S., Rust C. and Gibbs, G. (1994) *Strategies for Diversifying Assessment in Higher Education.* The Oxford Centre for Staff Development
Freeman, M. (1994) Peer assessment by groups of group work *Assessment and Evaluation in Higher Education* Vol. 20, no. 3.
Goodlad, S. and Hirst B. (1989) *Peer Tutoring: A Guide to Learning and Teaching.* London: Kogan Page.
Orsmond, P., Merry, S. and Reiling, K. (1996) The importance of marking criteria in the use of peer assessment, *Assessment and Evaluation*, Vol. 21, no. 3.
Topping, K. (1988) *The Peer Tutoring Handbook: Promoting Co-operative Learning.* Beckenham: Croom Helm.

7

Your Continuing Professional Development

CHAPTER OUTLINE

This chapter examines the various roles carried out by the teacher (7.1) then looks at the different ways in which self-evaluation can take place (7.2). Ideas on how your management of time can be improved are suggested (7.3), and then techniques of evaluation by peers are introduced (7.4). The importance of teams and their development is emphasised (7.5). The various styles of management within teaching and training are explored (7.6), and finally aspects of appraisal, fundamental to the development of teaching, training and learning, are considered (7.7).

The FENTO Standards addressed in this chapter

Many aspects of Key Area G – Reflecting upon and evaluating one's own performance and planning future practice – are addressed in this chapter. For example:

G1 Evaluate one's own practice

(a) identify where and how their subject or vocational area fits within the organisation and the wider FE sector

(b) consider their own professional practice in relation to the major influences upon FE

(e) conduct a critical evaluation of their own teaching by eliciting, valuing and using feedback from learners, other teachers, managers and external evaluators

(f) evaluate their own key skills against what is required in their teaching

(i) create and use opportunities to question their own practice and to seek audits of their competence from others, as appropriate

(j) use evaluations to improve their own and their team's effectiveness

Critical understanding and essential knowledge

- their current role and the knowledge and skills required to carry it out
- what constitutes relevant evidence of teachers' own practice and how to interpret it
- ways of addressing teachers' own development needs

In addition, Key Area H – Meeting professional requirements – is addressed, for example:
work effectively with others to benefit learners

7.1 The roles of the teacher

Teaching is obviously the central role, embracing not only classroom-based teaching and learning processes but all of the allied activities crucial to the teaching–learning process which include:

- course design and redevelopment
- updating and developing subject knowledge and expertise
- assessing and moderating learners' work.

In addition to this key role of teaching, the teacher will inevitably have a range of other duties and activities, which tend to increase with experience. Figure 7.1 illustrates these other roles of the teacher and their relationship with one another.

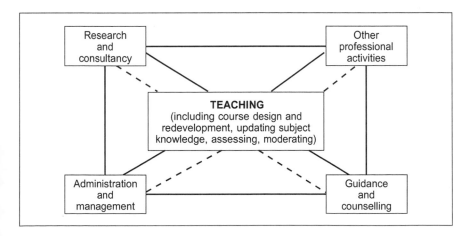

Figure 7.1 The various roles of the teacher, indicating their relationship with one another

The central role of teaching has been addressed previously, particularly in Chapters 2 and 4, and is considered further in 7.2. Some aspects of the other roles are considered below.

Administration and management
Are you involved in all/some of the following:

- managing, attending meetings
- keeping records (of learners, resources and finances)
- marketing courses and programmes, and other forms of income generation
- liaison with external organisations, employers etc.
- membership of working parties, steering committees?

Guidance and counselling
These activities, which are more or less synonymous and work hand in glove, provide a service to your learners, both during a course and at transition points; for example, when the learners are entering your course and on exit.

The Further Education Unit (1987) identified several guidance skills which you need to practise and develop:

- *Taking action* – working on behalf of the learner by speaking for him/her to others.
- *Advising* – giving suggestions to learners from a range of alternative possibilities.
- *Informing* – giving learners information based on a firm foundation of knowledge in a specific area; for example, careers information within your area of experience and expertise.
- *Counselling* – helping the learner to work through personal problems or issues in a positive, constructive manner.

To develop these skills, you will need constantly to update the following:

- your knowledge of relevant and local organisations and agencies
- other people and services within your own organisation to whom you can refer
- changes in the legislation in key areas; for example, health and safety, equal opportunities, student funding, international students.

Research and consultancy
Some questions to consider are given below:

- Are you involved in personal or group research in your own particular subject area or in teaching and learning?
- Are you responsible for supervising or advising on the research of others?
- Are you aware of the opportunities and funding provision for research within

your own organisation?

- Are you conversant with local, national and international funding agencies for research?
- Are commercial/industrial/public sector organisations aware of your expertise which could be used in a consultancy capacity?
- Have you investigated the scope for collaborative research with commercial/industrial/public sector organisations?

Other professional activities

These could include:

- trade union activities
- exchange activities with other educational or non-educational organisations within the UK or abroad
- making inputs to local and national media
- acting as an external assessor/moderator/verifier/adviser/inspector for other educational organisations
- producing educational materials; for example, books, computer software, videos, artefacts etc.

7.2 Self-evaluation

Many of the course evaluation methods discussed in 3.6 (through survey, observation, documents, statistics) can be used in self-evaluation, with the focus moved from an emphasis on a particular course to an analysis of your own performance over a range of activities, of which teaching will be the dominant area of interest.

As well as you yourself, there will be necessarily other 'stakeholders' involved, notably your learners and colleagues, and therefore as well as evaluation information based on your own self-perception, very helpful evaluative evidence can be generated by these other stakeholders. By collecting information from different stakeholders, the highly subjective stance which necessarily is associated with self-perception may be tempered.

Particularly useful ways of collecting evaluative information, whether based on your own perceptions or those of others, are:

- checklists
- questionnaires
- video recordings of teaching
- reflective diaries.

Some examples of simple yet effective checklists for self-completion are given in Figure 7.2, which focuses on three areas:

- attitudes to learners
- characteristics and actions relating to subject matter
- personal characteristics.

These three areas very much overlap and interrelate, but separation into distinct categories will help to sharpen your focus.

Attitude to learners			Characteristics and actions relating to subject matter			Personal characteristics		
	Yes	No		Yes	No		Yes	No
Friendly Respectful Encouraging Co-operative Placid Tolerant Impartial Supportive Informal Welcoming Fair Sensitive to their needs Positive Committed Approachable			Knowledgeable Enthusiastic Up-to-date Confident Detailed Imaginative Logically ordered Inspiring Coherenly structured Thought-provoking			Lively Courteous Humorous Flexible Decisive Warm Confident Polite		

Figure 7.2 Self-evaluation checklists

TASK ONE

- What other attitudes and characteristics would you add to the checklists in Figure 7.2?

- Obtain your learners' views on your attitudes and characteristics by letting them complete the checklists in Figure 7.2. What differences exist sbetween your learners' views and your own?

Figures 3.11, 3.13 and 3.14, designed for learners' and colleagues' evaluation of your teaching, can be modified for your own self-completion. Figure 7.3 shows an example of a self-evaluation checklist, focusing on the key aspects of teaching.

	Yes	No
Am I clear about the aims of my teaching? Do my students know what the aims are? Are the aims relevant to the needs of my learners? Do I make the learning environment as pleasant as possible? Do I know my teaching subject matter thoroughly? Is the subject matter presented in a logical order? Does it have a coherent structure? Do I make use of relevant examples? Do I use my students' experience and expertise? Do I ensure that every student is involved in active learning? Do I use appropriate assessment methods? Do I monitor students' learning in a variety of ways? Do I use a variety of audio-visual aids? Do I enjoy my teaching? Can I improve certain aspects of my teaching?		

Figure 7.3 A further self-evaluation checklist

Video recordings are very helpful in the self-evaluation of teaching. Entire sessions or segments can be recorded, and analysed afterwards either by yourself or with the assistance of colleagues and learners who can give an added dimension to the analysis. The example questionnaires in Chapter 3 (Figure 3.11, part 4; Figure 3.13; Figure 3.14; Figure 3.15) can be used for self-evaluation while reviewing your video-recorded teaching session, as can Figure 7.3.

Some questions to ask yourself while analysing your video recording include:

- Was there continuity with previous teaching sessions?
- Were the aims clear?
- Could instructions and questions be expressed more effectively?
- How much time was spent interacting with individual learners and groups of learners?
- Could time be used more effectively during the session?
- Could non-verbal behaviour (including body language) be improved in any way?
- Was the varying rate of progress of individual learners and groups of learners addressed effectively?
- Did the learners appear interested and enthusiastic?
- Was the session concluded in a positive and unhurried way?
- Was reference made to the following and future sessions?

Reflective diaries are helpful in noting a range of evaluative issues and questions, such as:

- Which teaching–learning techniques went particularly well/badly?
- Which teaching materials seemed to be particularly stimulating?
- Which subject matter seemed to cause most difficulty among learners?
- Which topics took more time than anticipated?
- Which assessment tasks were particularly valuable?
- Which resources were found to be most stimulating and valuable?

If reflective diaries are kept in a systematic way, they will help you to sharpen your awareness of the key aspects of your work to focus upon, and over time, such analysis and reflection will lead to an improvement in the many aspects of your work.

A useful self-evaluation technique, originally used for evaluation of organisations, is SWOT analysis, 'SWOT' being made from the initial letters of Strengths, Weaknesses, Opportunities, Threats. It has, over the years, been applied to a wide range of evaluation situations, including the evaluation of individuals, giving four clear emphases to focus upon (see **Task Two**).

TASK TWO

Five aspects of your role have been identified below. List your strengths, weaknesses, opportunities and threats that you think relate to each area.

Aspect of your role	Strengths	Weaknesses	Opportunities	Threats
Teaching				
Administration and management				
Guidance and counselling				
Research and consultancy				
Other professional activities				

List how your weaknesses can be addressed and minimised.

7.3 Managing time

Time is one of our most valuable resources and most of us can improve our effectiveness by improving the ways in which we manage and use time.

Task Three, based on an exercise in Everard and Morris (1996), helps you to think about how you spend your time at present, how ideally you would like to spend it, and how you can manage your time more effectively.

TASK THREE

(a) Using the activities shown in column 1 of the activity time sheet, and others you feel are applicable, estimate the amount of your time you have spent on each activity during the past week, expressed as a percentage of your total working time. Use column 2 (Actual) for listing your estimates.

(b) Use column 3 to fill in the time allocation you ideally would like to spend on each activity over the next month.

(c) Which activities show the greatest discrepancy between 'actual' and 'ideal' in terms of time commitment?

(d) What realistic changes can you introduce to try to achieve your ideal time allocation to each activity?

(e) What can colleagues do to help you to achieve your ideal time allocation to each activity?

1. Activity	2. Actual time spent %	3. Ideal time spent %
Classroom teaching Group tutorials Individual tutorials Lesson preparation Marking learners' work Liaising with colleagues Attending meetings Writing letters General administration Interviews Liaison with external organisations Travel Others		

Some ways of improving time management include the following:

- keeping lists of jobs to be done each day
- putting these jobs in an order of priority
- delegating tasks (taking care not to overload other people!)
- being realistic about what you can achieve each day
- having 'green time' and 'red time', i.e. time when you can see other people, and time when you can't
- working closely in a team and using the attributes of other team members to save time (see Figure 7.4)
- putting definite limits to the length of meetings
- learning to say 'no' without being offensive.

7.4 Evaluation by peers

Forming a partnership or paired observation with a colleague for evaluation purposes can be a rewarding experience with many advantages. Some of these have been outlined by Holly and Southworth (1989) and are included, with other aspects, below:

- Observing the behaviour of other teachers may make a teacher more aware of his/her own teaching.
- It enables colleagues to share ideas.
- Teachers rarely see their peers teaching.
- It helps to break down barriers between classrooms and therefore alleviates the problem of isolation.
- Team spirit, trust, collaboration can develop over time.
- As it is both teacher-focused and learner-focused, it is learning-focused.
- It provides stimulation arising from discussion, reflection, analysis and collaborative action.
- Certain detailed elements of teaching – for example, asking questions, listening to responses, non-verbal communication – can be focused upon, and systematically sharpened and honed.

The evaluation questionnaires and checklists exemplified in Chapter 3 (Figures 3.11, 3.13 and 3.14 and earlier in this chapter Figure 7.3) can be useful in establishing the criteria for a peer to focus upon. Discussion with a colleague can, of course, be a very powerful learning experience prior to or after peer observation.

TASK FOUR

With a colleague, draw up a list of criteria to be used in a peer observation of one of your teaching sessions.

7.5 Team building

Teaching is nowadays very team-focused, and most teachers come into contact with other colleagues on either a formal or informal basis, or both.

It is helpful to know what role each of us can play most effectively in a team, and to have some knowledge of how teams develop over time.

Belbin (1993) has carried out much research on team composition, with a view to predicting the effectiveness of team performance. Balance in a team is a crucial element and Belbin has identified the different types necessary for the ideal team (see Figure 7.4). A team with all of these types does not guarantee success, but not having one or more of the types does increase the possibility of failure.

TASK FIVE

Study Figure 7.4. Which type of team member do you consider yourself to be?

Think of the different teams you belong to. Do the teams have all the different types of team member?

Are you able to fulfil your ideal role with the teams you belong to?

Roles and descriptions – team-role contribution	Allowable weaknesses
Plant: Creative, imaginative, unorthodox. Solves difficult problems.	Ignores details. Too preoccupied to communicate effectively.
Resource investigator: Extrovert, enthusiastic, communicative. Explores opportunities. Develops contacts.	Over-optimistic. Loses interest once initial enthusiasm has passed.
Co-ordinator: Mature, confident, a good chairperson. Clarifies goals, promotes decision-making, delegates well.	Can be seen as manipulative. Delegates personal work.
Shaper: Challenging, dynamic, thrives on pressure. Has the drive and courage to overcome obstacles.	Can provoke others. Hurts people's feelings.
Monitor evaluator: Sober, strategic and discerning. Sees all options. Judges accurately.	Lacks drive and ability to inspire others. Overly critical.
Teamworker: Co-operative, mild, perceptive and diplomatic. Listens, builds, averts friction, calms the waters.	Indecisive in crunch situations. Can be easily influenced.
Implementer: Disciplined, reliable, conservative and efficient. Turns ideas into practical actions.	Somewhat inflexible. Slow to respond to new possibilities.
Completer: Painstaking, conscientious, anxious. Searches out errors and omissions. Delivers on time.	Inclined to worry unduly. Reluctant to delegate. Can be a nit-picker.
Specialist: Single-minded, self-starting, dedicated. Provides knowledge and skills in rare supply.	Contributes on only a narrow front. Dwells on technicalities. Overlooks the 'big picture'.

Figure 7.4. The roles and descriptions of ideal team members (based on Belbin, 1993)

As teams develop, they tend to show different characteristics. Tuckman (1965) has identified five stages of progression: forming, storming, norming, reforming and performing (Figure 7.5).

An understanding of team development, such as that outlined by Tuckman, is helpful since it indicates to us, for example, the need to emphasise the importance in the forming stage of getting to know other team members, of examining the

FORMING (Ritual sniffing)	STORMING (Infighting)	NORMING (Experimenting)	REFORMING (Effectiveness)	PERFORMING (Maturity & excellence)
TEAM DEVELOPMENT ➤				
Unclear objectives	Lack of unity	Question performance	Change/re-affirm goals and objectives	Leadership according to situation
Central authority	Lack of method	Review goals and objectives	Restructure	Flexibility
Conforming	Relationships significant	Review team and individual performance	Change/confirm roles	Openness
Caution	Cliques			Effective boundary management
Feelings hidden	Strength and weaknesses known	Open up risky issues	Improve working methods	
Anxiety				Individual and team needs compatible
Poor listening	Leadership questioned	Question assumptions and commitment	Build on strengths	
Little care for others	Tension, anger, cynicism, scapegoats		Resolve weaknesses	Risk-taking
Initial pairing		Leadership discussed	Develop team	Pride
Weaknesses covered up	Confusion	Deal with animosities	Willingness to experiment	Excitement
Enthusiasm vs wait and see	Failure			Learning
	Hidden agendas	Greater clarity	Better listening	Achievement
	Disillusion	Relief	Involvement	Trust
	Team's needs emerge			

Figure 7.5. Stages in team development (based on Tuckman, 1965)

purpose of the team, and of identifying existing skills and knowledge. At this early stage, it is therefore essential not to jump to conclusions or effect changes too quickly. Similarly, the characteristics identified at each stage by Tuckman help us to understand why team members behave in certain ways at various stages of development.

Teams do not necessarily move in a linear fashion through all stages. Some may, for example, reach the storming stage but move no further. Some move forward then backwards, then forward again.

TASK SIX

• Consider the teams you belong to. Which stages are they at?

• Is any team stuck at any particular stage?

• What particular characteristics are hindering further progression?

7.6 Styles of management

The style of management affects the climate, ethos or atmosphere of the organisation in which we work. It is, therefore, important to be aware of some of the main styles of management and the characteristics of each style, so that we understand more fully why certain decisions are taken within our organisation and why some aspects of teaching and learning are emphasised at the expense of others.

A wide variety of styles of management exist, but most are variants and extensions of the premise that every manager has two main concerns:

- to achieve results ('task' oriented)
- to develop relationships ('people' oriented).

Blake and Mouton (1964) developed these management dimensions into their 'management grid', a nine cell by nine cell grid which enables different management styles to be located (see Figure 7.6). Some of the characteristics of the management styles are given below:

1.9 on the grid Caring:

- cares about people
- wants to be liked
- avoids open conflict
- 'if the organisation is happy, that is all that matters'
- praises achievement (even flatters)
- glosses over poor performance
- favours 'management by committee'
- is helpful.

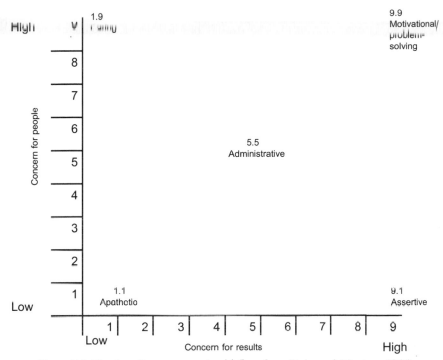

Figure 7.6. The 9 × 9 management grid (based on Blake and Mouton, 1964)

9.9 on the grid Motivational/problem-solving

- agrees goals and expects achievement
- monitors performance against goals
- helps staff to find solutions to poor performance
- faces up to conflict calmly
- agrees and monitors action plans
- involves staff in decisions which affect them
- delegates clearly
- takes decisions as and when needed.

5.5 on the grid Administrative

- goes by the book
- maintains the existing system
- conscientious rather than creative or innovative
- steady.

1.1 on the grid Apathetic

People whose concern is neither for results nor for people are often frustrated, disillusioned or feel under threat. They may respond either 'passively' or by taking part in 'political' activity.

Passive behaviour:

- does no more than is required
- resists change; becomes slack if not checked
- blames other people for creating poor conditions.

Political behaviour:

- is very concerned about status
- is quick to criticise
- draws attention to the faults of others.

9.1 on the grid Assertive:

- wants things done his or her way
- 'tells' rather than 'listens'
- doesn't worry too much about other people's feelings or opinions
- aggressive if challenged.

TASK SEVEN

- Consider the management tasks you carry out as part of your job. Which management style do you adopt most frequently?

- What factors influence you most in adopting this management style?

- Thinking of your own 'managers', which styles do they adopt?

- Which style do you prefer your 'managers' to adopt?

7.7 Appraisal and the quest for quality

Staff appraisal systems are now well established in most organisations. The ultimate aim of appraisal is to raise the quality of the work and the working environment of the individual, and of the individual's organisation, and ultimately student learning and achievement.

The best organised staff appraisal schemes can result in a number of benefits, as outlined by Poster and Poster (1993). For the individual, appraisal systems:

- encourage self-development and personal initiative
- improve self-confidence and self-esteem
- give a sense of purpose through specifying clear goals
- reduce alienation and resentment through open discussion.

For the organisation, such systems:

- direct individual effort into organisational goals
- help to communicate organisational aims to all staff
- help to identify where changes are needed
- contribute to long-term planning

For both the individual and the organisation, appraisal schemes:

- help to build morale
- provide a facility whereby individual effort can be recognised, even when no financial reward can be given
- develop the means whereby an individual can influence the organisation
- encourage better communication, and the creation of a more open style of management.

Different approaches to staff appraisal can be adopted, but in most organisations concerned with education and training, emphasis on professional development is probably the most relevant and successful. Such a professional development approach towards appraisal shows characteristics such as:

- the identification of the criteria to be considered by all parties involved in the appraisal
- an atmosphere of support, trust, openness and dialogue
- a spirit of co-operation and collaboration
- the importance of team work
- an emphasis on agreeing amicably a programme with shared responsibility for the achievement of goals
- the encouragement of the constant reflection by the individual upon his/her work, progress, development and goals.

Many of the criteria, information and techniques outlined in 7.2 and 7.4 can be used in appraisal.

In addition, a very common method to form part of an appraisal scheme is the appraisal interview by an individual's manager. Such interviews are most successful where the appraisee identifies the areas for discussion and communicates these to the appraiser in advance of the interview. A helpful structure for the interview is to raise issues relating to:

(a) the past year
(b) the coming year
(c) long-term career plan.

Under these headings, the following questions can provide a helpful focus for the appraisal interview:

(a) The past year
- How far have I achieved the goals of the past year?
- Are there any areas in which I need help or training?
- What aspects of my teaching do I enjoy the most?
- What obstacles restricted my teaching to my full potential?
- How can these obstacles be overcome?
- How did others see me in my work?
- What could I have done better?

(b) The coming year
- What do I hope to build on, that was positive, from last year?
- What are my goals this year?
- How can the organisation support me in achieving these goals?
- Are there any courses or conferences I want to attend?
- What do I want to do for my own personal development?

(c) Long-term career plans
- How do I see my career progressing?
- Where do I see myself in five years' time?
- Which areas of responsibility would I be interested in?
- Which staff development/training areas would I be interested in?
- Can any of my skills and abilities be used in a more effective way?

TASK EIGHT

What other questions would you add to those above to be asked at your own appraisal interview?

Although the cost of appraisal, in both time and money, can be very high, if carried out in a positive, non-threatening, fair and comprehensive manner it can be a highly effective mechanism for improving teaching quality, increasing job satisfaction and the enhancing learning experience.

Summary

In this chapter we have considered a variety of different aspects of continuing professional development.

The varied roles which a teacher undertakes have been identified, and self- and peer evaluation techniques helpful for the reflection upon and development of expertise and performance have been reviewed.

The importance of using time more efficiently has been emphasised and the ways in which teams evolve and develop and the different contributions and attributes of team members have been focused upon.

Various styles of management have been highlighted, and the contributions which appraisal schemes can make to improvement in the quality of performance have been considered.

Teaching the post-16 learner is a challenging job, and this chapter has indicated a variety of ways in which constant reflection can lead to the enhancement of quality of the learning experience, both for the learner and for the teacher.

References and further reading

Belbin, R.M. (1963) *Team Roles at Work*. Oxford: Butterworth-Heinemann.

Blake, R.R. and Mouton, J.S. (1964) *The Managerial Grid: Key Orientations for Achieving Production Through People*. Houston: Gulf.

Everard, K.B. and Morris, G. (1996) *Effective School Management*. London: Paul Chapman.

Further Education Funding Council (1999) *Professional Development in Further Education*. Coventry: FEFC.

Further Education Unit (1987) *A Self Profile for Continuing Professional Development*. London: Further Education Unit.

Holly, P. and Southworth G. (1989) *The Developing School*. London: Falmer.

Poster, C. and Poster, D. (1991) *Teacher Appraisal: A Guide to Training*. London: Routledge.

Tuckman, B.W. (1965) Development sequences in small groups, *Psychological Bulletin*, Vol. 63.

Appendix:
Teaching Styles Questionnaire

In Chapter 2 it was suggested that you assess your preferred teaching style by the use of a teaching style questionnaire. The questionnaire was developed by Dixon and Woolhouse (1996) based on the learning styles questionnaire developed by Honey and Mumford (1986).

To do this you need to:

(a)   Complete the questionnaire (pp. 139–142) by answering each question. See the instructions at the beginning of the questionnaire. Answer these 80 questions quickly – the response should be your immediate reaction, rather than a considered answer.

(b)   Complete the scoring sheet by ticking the numbers you put a tick besides in the questionnaire and then total the ticks (p. 143).

(c)   Plot the four scores from the list onto the arms of the cross and then join them up to form a 'diamond' (p. 144). An example of a score sheet and a 'diamond' is given on pp. 145–146.

This may show you which style you have a preference for. If you have a strong preference for one or more styles, you might consider trying to adapt to include teaching strategies which are preferred by the other styles to appeal to all learners. See pp. 147–148 of Appendix for possible ways of doing this.

If there is no pronounced preference this means you are probably a 'well-balanced' teacher and already use strategies which are preferred by all the four styles.

TEACHING STYLES QUESTIONNAIRE

This questionnaire has been developed to discover if you have a preferred teaching style(s). You have probably developed 'inclinations' towards the particular style(s) of teaching that help you to be more efficient in your teaching. Since it is common to be unaware of this, this questionnaire will help you to pinpoint your teaching preferences so that you are in a better position to select teaching methods which broaden your teaching styles.

There is no time limit to this questionnaire. It will probably take you 10–15 minutes. The accuracy of the results depends on how honest you can be. *There are no right or wrong answers.*

If you agree more than you disagree with a statement put a tick by it (✓). If you disagree more than you agree put a cross by it (✗). Be sure to mark each item with either a tick or a cross.

☐ 1   In teaching and education I have very strong beliefs about what is right and wrong, good and bad.

☐ 2   In a teaching situation I sometimes act without considering the possible consequences.

☐ 3   I tend to solve the problems that arise at work by using a step-by-step approach.

☐ 4   I believe that teachers are restricted by the more formal teaching methods and procedures.

☐ 5   I have a reputation amongst my students for saying what I think, simply and directly.

☐ 6   When teaching I often find that actions based on feelings are as sound as those based on careful thought and analysis.

☐ 7   I like it when I have time for thorough preparation and teaching of a subject.

☐ 8   I regularly question my students about their basic assumptions.

☐ 9   In teaching and education what matters most is whether something works in practice.

☐ 10   I actively seek out new teaching styles and strategies to try.

☐ 11   When I hear about a new idea or approach to education I often start working out how to apply it in practice.

☐ 12   I think that self-discipline such as planning and working to schedules, sticking to a fixed routine, etc. is important.

☐ 13   I take pride in teaching a subject area thoroughly.

☐ 14   I enjoy teaching the more logical and analytical students rather than the more spontaneous, 'irrational' students.

☐ 15   I take care over the interpretation of information/data available to me and avoid jumping to conclusions.

☐ 16   I like to answer students' questions by the careful weighing up of different alternatives.

☐ 17   I'm attracted to novel, unusual *ideas* about teaching and education rather than to the old tried and tested ones.

☐ 18   I prefer my lessons to follow a coherent pattern rather than be spontaneous and 'disorganised'.

☐ 19   I accept and stick to laid-down teaching procedures and strategies so long as I regard them as efficient.

☐ 20   I like to relate my teaching activities to a general principle.

☐ 21   In classroom discussions I like to get straight to the point.

☐ 22   I tend to have distant, rather formal relationships with my students.

☐ 23   I thrive on the challenge of tackling new and different subjects and students.

☐ 24   I enjoy teaching fun-loving, spontaneous students.

☐ 25   In the teaching situation I pay meticulous attention to detail before coming to a conclusion.

☐ 26   In lessons I find it difficult to produce ideas on impulse.

☐ 27   When giving lessons I believe in coming to the point immediately.

☐ 28   I am careful not to jump to conclusions about my students too quickly.

☐ 29   I prefer to have as many sources of teaching material as possible – the more information/data to consider the better.

☐ 30   Flippant students who don't take life seriously enough usually irritate me.

☐ 31   I like to hear my students' point of view before putting my own forward.

☐ 32   I tend to be open to my students about how I am feeling.

☐ 33   In classroom discussions I enjoy watching the manoeuvrings of my students.

☐ 34   During lessons I tend to respond to events on a spontaneous, flexible basis rather than adhere to a planned programme that I have prepared in advance.

☐ 35   When planning my teaching I tend to consider techniques such as self-evaluation, quality control, contingency planning, etc.

☐ 36   It worries me if I have to rush my preparation, teaching or marking in order to meet a tight schedule.

☐ 37   I tend to judge my students' ideas on their practical merits.

☐ 38   When dealing with quiet and introspective students I tend to feel uneasy.

☐ 39   I often get irritated by students who want to rush things.

☐ 40   It is more important to enjoy the present moment rather than to dwell upon the past or worry about the future.

☐ 41   I think that educational decisions based on a thorough analysis of all the information are sounder than those based upon intuition.

☐ 42   In my teaching work I tend to be a perfectionist who won't rest easy until things are tidy and fit into a rational scheme.

☐ 43   In classroom discussions I usually produce lots of spontaneous ideas for my students to consider.

☐ 44   To solve any problems during my lessons I put forward practical realistic ideas.

☐ 45   More often than not the 'rules' about teaching and education are there to be broken.

☐ 46   I prefer to stand back from a classroom situation and consider all the perspectives.

☐ 47   More often than not I see inconsistencies and weaknesses in my students' arguments.

☐ 48   On balance when talking to students I talk more than I listen.

☐ 49   I most often see better, more practical ways to get things done than my students.

☐ 50   I think that students' reports should be short and to the point.

☐ 51   In educational matters I belive that rational, logical thinking should win the day.

☐ 52   I tend to discuss the technical aspects of the syllabus with my students rather than engaging in social discussion.

☐ 53   I like students who approach things realistically rather than theoretically.

☐ 54   During my lessons I get impatient with irrelevances and digressions.

☐ 55   When I am preparing student handouts or writing a report I tend to produce lots of drafts before settling on the final version.

☐ 56   I am keen to try things out to see if they work in practice

☐ 57   I am always keen that my students reach answers via a logical approach.

☐ 58   I enjoy being a teacher because I enjoy being the one that talks a lot.

☐ 59   In my lessons I often find that I am the realist, keeping my students to the point and avoiding wild speculations.

☐ 60   I ponder many alternatives before making up my mind on an educational matter.

☐ 61   In discussion with my students I often find that I am the most dispassionate and objective.

☐ 62   In a classroom discussion I'm more likely to 'stay in the background' than to take the lead and do most of the teaching.

☐ 63   I like to be able to relate my current teaching activities to a longer-term 'bigger picture'.

☐ 64   When things go wrong with my teaching I am happy to shrug it off and 'put it down to experience'.

☐ 65   I tend to reject students' wild, spontaneous ideas as being impractical.

☐ 66   When giving a lesson it's best to think carefully before taking any action.

☐ 67   On balance when talking to students I do the listening rather than the talking.

☐ 68   I tend to be tough on students who find it difficult to adopt a logical approach.

☐ 69   In my teaching I generally believe that the end justifies the means.

☐ 70   I don't mind hurting students' feelings so long as it means they get their work done.

☐ 71   I often find the formality of having to follow specific teaching objectives and strategies stifling.

☐ 72   I like to put lots of life into my lessons.

☐ 73   In my lessons I do whatever is expedient to cover the syllabus.

☐ 74   I quickly get bored when teaching methodical and detailed subject areas.

☐ 75   I am keen for my students to explore the basic assumptions, principles and theories underpinning what they are learning.

☐ 76   I'm always interested to find out what my students think.

☐ 77   I like my lessons to be run on methodical lines, sticking to a laid-down teaching plan, etc.

☐ 78   During my lessons I steer clear of subjective or ambiguous topics.

☐ 79   I enjoy the drama and excitement of a crisis situation.

☐ 80   I expect that my students often find me insensitive to their feelings.

TEACHING STYLES QUESTIONNAIRE – SCORING

You score one point for each item you ticked (✓). There are no points for items you crossed (✗).

Simply indicate on the lists below which items were ticked.

2	7	1	5
4	13	3	9
6	15	8	11
10	16	12	19
17	25	14	21
23	28	18	27
24	29	20	35
32	31	22	37
34	33	26	44
38	36	30	49
40	39	42	50
43	41	47	53
45	46	51	54
48	52	57	56
58	55	61	59
64	60	63	65
71	62	68	69
72	66	75	70
74	67	77	73
79	76	78	80

Totals

Activist teacher	Reflector teacher	Theorist teacher	Pragmatist teacher

Plot the scores on the arms of the cross below for an indication of your preferred teaching style(s)

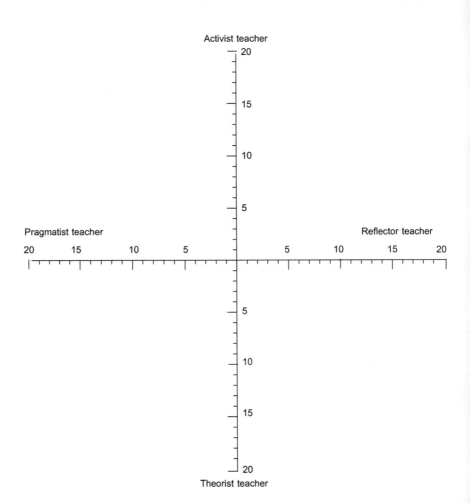

EXAMPLE TEACHING STYLES QUESTIONNAIRE – SCORING

You score one point for each item you ticked (✓). There are no points for items you crossed (✗).

Simply indicate on the lists below which items were ticked.

2	7 ✓	1 ✓	5 ✓
4 ✓	13 ✓	3	9
6 ✓	15 ✓	8	11
10 ✓	16	12	19
17	25 ✓	14 ✓	21 ✓
23 ✓	28 ✓	18	27
24 ✓	29	20	35
32	31 ✓	22	37
34 ✓	33 ✓	26	44 ✓
38 ✓	36 ✓	30 ✓	49
40 ✓	39 ✓	42 ✓	50
43	41 ✓	47	53
45 ✓	46 ✓	51	54 ✓
48	52	57	56
58	55 ✓	61	59
64 ✓	60 ✓	63	65
71 ✓	62 ✓	68	69
72 ✓	66	75	70
74	67 ✓	77	73
79 ✓	76	78	80 ✓

Totals	**13**	**15**	**4**	**5**
	Activist teacher	Reflector teacher	Theorist teacher	Pragmatist teacher

Plot the scores on the arms of the cross below for an indication of your preferred teaching style(s)

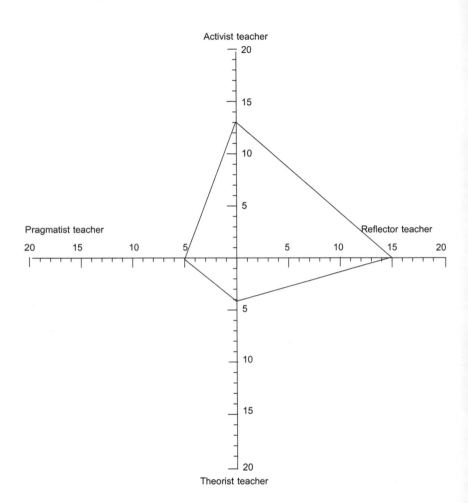

Developing teaching methods to fit learning Styles

As teachers there is a tendency for us to favour methods which encourage learners who learn in similar ways to ourselves. This is great for our strengths. It is helpful, though, to look particularly at developing methods favouring learning in 'quadrants' where we are not so strong.

To develop Reflective Observation

How effectively do I:

* Actively encourage students to ask questions?
* Put unusual situations to students and encourage speculation?
* Regularly give students a chance to think creatively about my subject?
* Give credit for intuition?
* Set exercises which encourage speculation?
* Set a mood suitable for imaginative work by the way I communicate with students?
* Ask open-ended questions and encourage divergent thinking approving
  – fluency (number of responses – no matter how diverse)?
  – individuality (rarity of answer)?
  – flexibility (the ability to think about different aspects of a problem)?

To develop Abstract Conceptualisation

How to effectively do I:

* Use conceptual models to simplify my subject?
* Present the necessary factual base and concepts of my subject in a clear and interesting manner?
* Encourage accuracy of recall?
* Place value on students demonstrating understanding of concepts?
* Value logical reasoning?
* Encourage deductive reasoning?
* Encourage students to look for patterns and categorise knowledge?
* Encourage students to be receptive to new ideas by the way in which I introduce them in my teaching?

To develop Active Experimentation

How effectively do I:

* Encourage skill acquisition through practical exercises? (Physical/speaking/listening/observational etc.)
* Use exercises designed to promote skills – or is their development a by-product?
* Use exercises to develop specific skills, i.e. is there skill discrimination?

- Test skill acquisition?
- Emphasise the relevance of the content?
- Teach exercises which are designed to test theories?
- Encourage students to plan their work?
- Encourage experimental design?
- Teach students to record their work through a variety of note-making techniques?
- Set comprehension exercises designed to develop analytical skills?
- Teach specific learning skills, e.g. listening, recall etc.?
- Encourage practical work through the manner in which I relate to students?

To develop Concrete Experience
How effectively do I:

- Allow students to follow their own diversions?
- Encourage initiative and independence?
- Encourage skills, concepts and knowledge to be used in a variety of situations, (i.e. out of their original context)?
- Allow students to make mistakes and follow 'blind alleys' as part of the learning process?
- Make students critically examine and test their concepts and so encourage them to structure their own knowledge?
- Give credit to 'gut' feelings which may be correct but have no basis in logic?
- Anticipate the resource implications of student-led learning?
- Use my own communication skills to encourage initiative in students?

Glossary

APL	Accreditation of Prior Learning
APEL	Accreditation of Prior Experiential Learning
BTEC	Business and Technology Education Council (now EDEXCEL)
DES	Department of Education and Science (became DFE)
DFE	Department for Education (now DfEE)
DfEE	Department for Education and Employment
DSS	Department of Social Security
EDEXCEL	Education Excellence (formerly BTEC and ULEAC)
EOSC	Employment Occupational Standards Council
FE	Further Education
FEDA	Further Education Development Agency
FEFC	Further Education Funding Council
FENTO	Further Education National Training Organisation
FEU	Further Education Unit (now FEDA)
GCSE	General Certificate of Secondary Education
GNVQ	General National Vocational Qualification
NCVQ	National Council for Vocational Qualifications (now QCA)
NVQ	National Vocational Qualification
OCR	Oxford, Cambridge and RSA Examinations
OFSTED	Office for Standards in Education
OHP	overhead projector
QAA	Quality Assurance Agency for Higher Education
QCA	Qualifications and Curriculum Authority (formerly NCVQ and SCAA)'
RSA	Royal Society of Arts (now part of OCR)
SCAA	Schools Curriculum and Assessment Authority
SVQ	Scottish Vocational Qualification
TDLB	Training and Development Lead Body (now EOSC)
ULEAC	University of London Examinations and Assessment Council (now EDEXCEL)
VCR	video cassette recorder

Useful Addresses

The following organisations provide some helpful publications and other resources related to teaching the post-16 learner.

Associated Examining Board (AEB), (Assessment and Qualification Alliance, AQA), Stag Hill House, Guildford, Surrey GU2 5XJ. Phone: (01483) 506506.

Association of Teachers and Lecturers (ATL), 7 Northumberland Street, London WC2N 5DA. Phone: (020) 7930 6441.

Association of University Teachers (AUT), Egmont House, 25–31 Tavistock Place, London WC1H 9UT. Phone: (020) 7670 9700.

The Basic Skills Agency, Commonwealth House, 1–19 New Oxford Street, London WC1A 1NU. Phone: (020) 7405 4017.

BBC Education, White City, 201 Wood Lane, London W12 7TS. Phone: (020) 8746 1111.

The British Education Communications and Technology Agency (BECTa), Milburn Hill Road, Science Park, Coventry CV4 7JJ. Phone: (024) 7641 6994.

Careers and Occupational Information Centre (COIC), PO Box 298A, Thames Ditton, Surrey KT7 0ZS. Phone: (020) 8957 5030.

Channel 4 Learning, PO Box 100, Warwick CV34 6TZ. Phone: (01926) 436464.

City and Guilds of London Institute (CGLI), 1 Giltspur Street, London EC1A 9DD. Phone: (020) 7294 2468.

Department for Education and Employment (DfEE), Sanctuary Buildings, Great Smith Street, London SW1P 3BT. Phone: (020) 7925 5000.

DfEE Publications, PO Box 5050, Sherwood Park, Annesley, Nottingham NG15 0DJ. Phone: 0845 602 2260.

Edexcel BTEC, Edexcel Foundation, Stewart House, 32 Russell Square, London WC1B 5DN. Phone: (020) 7393 4500.

Equal Opportunities Commission, Overseas House, Quay Street, Manchester M3 3HN. Phone: (0161) 833 9244.

Further Education Development Agency (FEDA), Citadel Place, Tinworth Street, London SE11 SEH. Phone: (020) 7840 5400.

Further Education Funding Council for England (FEFC), Cheylesmore House,

Quinton Road, Coventry CV1 2WT. Phone: (024) 7686 3000.
Further Education National Training Organisation (FENTO), c/o Association of Colleges, Centre Point, 103 New Oxford Street, London WC1A 1DU. Phone: (020) 7637 3919.
Further Education Research Network (FERN), FERN Centre, Scraptoft Campus, De Montfort University, Leicester LE7 8SU. Phone: (0116) 257 7888.
Higher Education Funding Council for England (HEFCE), Northavon House, Coldharbour Lane, Bristol BS16 1QD. Phone: (0117) 931 7317.
Institute of Learning and Teaching in Higher Education (ILT), Genesis 3, Innovation Way, York Science Park, Heslington, York YO10 5DQ. Phone: (01904) 434222.
Institute of Careers Guidance (ICG), 27a Lower High Street, Stourbridge, West Midlands DY8 1TA. Phone (01384) 376 6464.
Institute of Management, Management House, Cottingham Road, Corby, Northants NN17 1TT. Phone (01536) 204222.
Institute of Personnel and Development (IPD), IPD House, 35 Camp Road, Wimbledon, London SW19 4UX. Phone: (020) 8971 9000.
Investors in People UK Ltd (IiP), 7–10 Chandos Street, London W1M 9DE. Phone: (020) 7467 1900.
London Chamber of Commerce and Industry Examinations Board (LCCI), 112 Station Road, Sidcup, Kent DA15 7BJ. Phone: (020) 8302 0261.
Management Charter Initiative (MCI), 10–12 Russell Square, London WC1B 5BZ. Phone: (020) 7872 9000.
National Advisory Council for Education and Training Targets (NACETT), 222 Gray's Inn Road, London WC1X 8HL. Phone: (020) 7211 5012.
National Association of Teachers in Further and Higher Education (NATFHE), 27 Britannia Street, London WC1X 9JP. Phone: (020) 7837 3636.
National Foundation for Educational Research (NFER), The Mere, Upton Park, Slough, Berkshire SL1 2DQ. Phone: (01753) 574123.
National Grid for Learning (NGfL), c/o BECTa, Milburn Hill Road, Science Park, Coventry CV4 7JJ. Phone: (024) 7641 6994.
National Institute of Adult Continuing Education (NIACE), 21 De Montfort Street, Leicester LE1 7GE. Phone: (0116) 204 4200.
National Institute for Careers Education and Counselling (NICEC), Sheraton House, Castle Park, Cambridge CB3 0AX. Phone: (01223) 460277.
National Open College Network (NOCN), University of Derby, Kedleston Road, Derby DE22 1GB. TPhone: (01332) 622712.
National Training Organisations National Council, 10 Meadowcourt, Amos Road, Sheffield S9 1BX. Phone: (0114) 261 9926.
Northern Council for Further Education (VCFE), Portland House, New Bridge Street, Newcastle upon Tyne NE1 8AN. Phone: (0191) 201 3100.
Northern Examinations and Assessment Board (NEAB), (Assessment and

Qualifications Alliance, AQA), Devas Street, Manchester M15 6EX. Phone: (0161) 953 1180.

Office for Standards in Education (OFSTED), Alexandra House, 33 Kingsway, London WC2B 6SE. Phone: (020) 7421 6800.

The Open University, Walton Hall, Milton Keynes MK7 6AA. Phone: (01908) 274066.

Oxford, Cambridge and RSA Examinations (OCR), 1 Regent Street, Cambridge CB2 1GG. Phone: (01223) 552552.

Pitman Qualifications (PE1), 1 Giltspur Street, London EC1A 9DD. Phone: (020) 7294 2471.

Qualifications and Curriculum Authority (QCA), 83 Piccadilly, London W1J 8QA. Phone: (020) 7509 5555.

Qualifications Curriculum and Assessment Authority for Wales, Castle Building. Womanby Street, Cardiff CF1 9SX. Phone: (029) 2037 5400.

The Quality Assurance Agency for Higher Education (QAA), Southgate House, Southgate Street, Gloucester GL1 5UB. Phone: (01452) 557000.

Royal Society of Arts Examinations Board (RSA), Westwood Way, Coventry CV4 8HS. Phone: (024) 7647 0033.

Scottish Qualifications Authority, 24 Douglas Street, Glasgow G2 7NQ. Phone: (0141) 248 7900.

Skill (National Bureau for Students with Disabilities), Chapter House, Crucifix Lane, London SE1 3JW. Phone: (020) 7450 0620.

Skills and Enterprise Network, DfEE, Moorfoot, Sheffield S1 4PQ. Phone: (0114) 259 4037.

Teacher Training Agency (TTA), Portland House, Stag Place, London SW1E STT. Phone: (020) 7925 3754.

The Higher Education Training Organisation (THETO), Ingram House, 65 Wilkinson Street, Sheffield S10 2GJ. Phone: (0114) 222 1340.

Trades Union Congress (TUC), Congress House, Great Russell Street, London WC1B 3LS. Phone: (020) 7636 4030.

Training and Enterprise Councils National Council, Westminster Tower, 3 Albert Embankment, London SE1 7SX. Phone: (020) 7735 0010.

UK Skills, 18 Park Square East, London NW1 4LH. Phone: (020) 7543 7488.

Universities and Colleges Admissions Service (UCAS), Fulton House, Jessop Avenue, Cheltenham, Gloucester GL50 3SH. Phone: (01242) 227788.

University for Industry Ltd (UfI), The Innovation Centre, 217 Portobello Street, Sheffield S1 4DP. Phone: (0114) 224 2999.

Welsh Joint Education Committee (WJEC), 245 Western Avenue, Cardiff CF5 2YX. Phone: (029) 2026 5000.

Workers' Educational Association (WEA), Temple House, 17 Victoria Park Square, London E2 9PB. Phone: (020) 8983 1515.

Index